Words of Praise for *The Leadership Game*

"The principles of winning with God are the same in life and sports. Coach Pastor Tom gives us the game plan in *The Leadership Game*."

—LOWELL 'BUD' PAXSON
Chairman, Paxson Communications Corporation, PAX TV

"A great coach will train you to do what you couldn't do before; motivate you to do what you thought you couldn't; and bring out the absolute best performance you are capable of—and then some! Tom Mullins is a great coach. *The Leadership Game* is a playbook for success written by an outstanding coach who knows how to get results!"

—PETER LOWE,
President and CEO
Get Motivated Business Seminars

"In an entertaining and refreshing way, Tom shares the secrets of winning coaches. As an analyst, my job is to say what I see and, this book scores. Touchdown, Coach!"

—SPENCER TILLMAN
CBS Sports, and author of Scoring In The Red Zone

"Tom reveals insights into the world of coaching that I have used and that you can use as a leader in your field. Join me and other champions on a winning journey through *The Leadership Game*."

—LARRY COKER
Head Football Coach, University of Miami Hurricanes, 2001 National Champions

"Tom Mullins is a man among men. He is leading one of the most dynamic congregations in America. I have observed first hand his leadership, and rejoice in it, and stand in awe of it. *The Leadership Game* will be an encouragement to any who want to make their lives count for Christ—whether they be young or old, male or female, pastor or layman. I fully commend it."

—ADRIAN ROGERS
Senior Pastor Emeritus, Bellevue Baptist Church, Memphis, Tennessee

"No matter the field or arena, Tom Mullins is a competitor. Tom understands what it is like to be a part of a team—in sport, business and life—and how to lead that team. I am certain that what you read in Tom's book will have something for everyone—even us old jocks."

—JACK NICKLAUS
Golf Legend

"Tom Mullins is a leader who practices the principles he teaches. *The Leadership Game* is creative, inspiring, and motivational. If you want to win in life and leadership, this is the book for you."

—DR. JACK GRAHAM
Pastor, Prestonwood Baptist Church, Plano, Texas

"Having been in professional baseball for 41 years as a Major League player, ESPN Broadcaster, Yankees Broadcaster and currently Florida Marlins Television Broadcaster, sports, leadership and motivation have been a big part of my life. Tom Mullins taps into some of the best coaches of our time and gets you ready to go out and take on all challenges."

—TOMMY HUTTON
Florida Marlins Television Broadcaster

"No matter if you lead parishioners, soldiers, employees, or football players; the principles of leadership are the same. Therefore, every leader will want to read *The Leadership Game* to learn the principles from the successful coaches and become a winner in their chosen professions."

—ELMER L. TOWNS
Vice President, Liberty University
Dean, School of Religion, Lynchburg, Virginia

"Dr. Thomas Mullins has been building winning teams for decades. *The Leadership Game* provides seven winning principles that will move you from the mundane to the momentous; from wondering what went wrong to winning consistently in the game of life. Read it. Learn it. Achieve it!"

—JAMES O. DAVIS
Cofounder/President/CEO
Global Pastors Network, Orlando, Florida

"*The Leadership Game* is an excellent resource full of both practical and inspiring insight. It is a must read for those who wish to become outstanding leaders."

—WILLIAM PUGH
President, Athletes in Action

"No one knows how to motivate a team to win more than a coach." And Tom Mullins's experience as a football coach and now a pastor has given him a unique ability to develop and lead winning teams."

CORWIN ANTHONY
AIA Pro Ministry, Miami Dolphins Chaplain

"The coaches that have contributed comments and insights regarding the key principles covered in this book are some of the finest ever in the game. When you combine these great coaches with the insights and vision of Tom Mullins, the result will surely be a great one."

—GLENN A. BLACKWOOD
Managing Director SER, Clark Consulting
Safety, Miami Dolphins (1979 to 1988), two-time Super Bowl champion

"Tom Mullins was an outstanding athlete and coach and understands well the principles of leadership. He demonstrates that on a daily basis in building one of America's premier churches. *The Leadership Game* will be a tremendous help to leaders and influencers throughout the country and ultimately around the world. This will be an outstanding opportunity to help all of us grow in our own leadership abilities. Thanks, Tom, for writing this book."

—DAVID R. HANNAH
Chairman & CEO of IMPACT XXI

"Tom Mullins has written the ultimate full-contact examination of leadership. He's provided us an all-access sideline pass that enables us to learn first-hand from seven of the most intense, highly effective, innovative leaders of men. By the way, I've been in a few huddles with Tom Mullins when the heat was on. Trust me—when he speaks, everyone listens. This book will be required reading for all the students at Student Leadership University."

—JAY STRACK
Founder/President, www.studentleadershp.net

"Tom Mullins is one of the greatest leaders I know. His new book, *The Leadership Game,* compiles winning principles from some of the greatest coaches who have ever lived. Don't miss their powerful and practical advice. This book will make you a winner."

—DR. JERRY FALWELL
Founder/Chancellor, Liberty University, Lynchburg, VA

"Tom Mullins is a coach's coach. He is a leader's leader. *The Leadership Game* will give you tools to help you be an effective leader, and a leader of leaders. I have had the privilege of working with five national championship teams. The 'Seven Coaching Principles' taught in this book are essential to building a team that can compete at the highest level."

—STEVE DEBARDELABEN, Athletes in Action
Team Chaplain with the Miami Hurricanes and Miami Heat

"As a business leader and owner of professional sports teams, I believe Tom has captured the secret of great leadership found through the approach of coaches. In today's market, whether you are leading a company or a professional sports franchise, you've got to become an effective coach and you have to know how to build great teams."

—JERRY COLANGELO
Chairman & CEO of Phoenix Suns and Chairman of Arizona Diamondbacks

"This book really motivated me and inspired me! Nobody wants a boss; everyone wants a coach. Coach Mullins is a true winner, and this is a 'must' for anyone wanting to win big."

—ART WILLIAMS
President and Founder, A.L. Williams

"If you want to be a winner and a great champion of life, *The Leadership Game* will help you achieve that goal. Not only is Pastor Tom a great champion but a true man of God. You will be inspired by his words and how they will help you in the game of life."

—GARY CARTER
Baseball Hall of Fame

"Whether I was playing at the University of Okalahoma or working in the US Congress, the principles I learned from my coaches on how to lead and build teams have been an essential foundation to my leadership approach in life. Tom's insights will help all of us become more effective leaders on any level."

—J.C. WATTS
Former U.S. Congressman,
Chairman of the J.C. Watts Companies

"Proven leaders write the best leadership books, which is why Tom Mullin's book, *The Leadership Game,* is a must read for aspiring leaders. It brings together leadership principles from some of the greatest leaders in America: coaches of championship football teams. The principles that Tom outlines in this book are proven to build extremely successful teams in athletics and in ministry, as evidenced not only by winning championships but by the impact that his church has on its city."

—TED HAGGARD
President of the National Association of Evangelicals,
and Senior Pastor of New Life Church in Colorado Springs.

The Leadership Game

Winning Principles from Eight National Champions

Tom Mullins

NELSON BUSINESS

A Division of Thomas Nelson Publishers

Since 1798

www.thomasnelson.com

Published in Nashville, Tennessee, by Thomas Nelson, Inc.

Nelson Books titles may be purchased in bulk for educational, business, fundraising,
or sales promotional use. For information, please e-mail
SpecialMarkets@ThomasNelson.com.

Library of Congress Cataloging-in-Publication Data

Mullins, Tom, 1945–
        The leadership game : seven winning principles from eight national cham-
pions / Tom Mullins.
            p. cm.
        Includes bibliographical references.
        ISBN: 0-7852-1254-X (hardcover)
        1. Leadership. 2. Sports teams. 3. Teams in the workplace.
        I. Title.
        HD57.7.M854 2005
        796'.068'4—dc22

                                                            2005015663

Printed in the United States of America

05 06 07 08 09 QW 5 4 3 2 1

In honor and memory of my grandfather, Thomas Jefferson Steenbergen . . . a gifted man and a great leader who had a profound influence on my life, I dedicate this book.

Out of his genuine love for God and people, he knew how to add value to others' lives and empower them to reach for the highest goals. He believed in me and always encouraged me to dream big. He led by example and always had a positive attitude that was infectious.

As I look back, I see his leadership has motivated and guided me to continually strive for excellence in all that I do. His leadership still has great impact today.

Contents

Foreword
Dr. John Maxwell

I've often said that the greatest way to be successful is to hang around successful people; like begets like. We encounter eight different coaches in *The Leadership Game* who only have one thing in common, and that is that they have won. They all have different backgrounds, different perspectives, different ideas, different thoughts, different ways to teach, and different personalities, but they all know how to win. And we have an opportunity, through *The Leadership Game,* to sit down with these winning coaches and observe who they are and how they did it so that we can replicate their principles of success in our own endeavors.

An important thing to remember as you read this book is that when you consider and process the different coaches' perspectives, you are going to find that there are some who are closer to you—as far as how they think—than others. We learn the most from people who are most like us. If this book just introduced the ideas and practices of one winning coach, it might leave some of us out in the cold, but because it has the ideas and practices of eight winning coaches we can read it knowing that there is something in here from one of the coaches that we can really receive.

Another thing that I think makes winning possible after reading this book is not only the fact that we have access to winning national coaches, but the fact that the person who wrote this book has been a winner in life himself. In other words, a winner is taking us to the winners. We're not going into this with somebody who doesn't understand the game of life himself. Tom has been successful on the football field, he has been successful in relationships with people, he has been successful in ministry . . . he has simply been successful.

Now, here's what I know about Tom. He has a great desire to help people win in the game of life. I know people who have won themselves but have no desire to share those thoughts, ideas, or secrets with others. However, Tom has that desire. In fact, because he has been a coach, he gets a bigger kick out of training other people in how to win than winning himself. He realized long ago that the win always comes to him if he has the ability and willingness to develop a winning team.

So as you start into this book, understand that the person who is most desirous of your success is Coach Tom Mullins. That is why he has taken the time to write this book. That is why he has taken the time to do the interviews. That is why he has taken the time and gone through the expense of making sure that what is written in this book is applicable to you.

Tom could have walked away from interviewing these eight national champions with success principles that would benefit only him. But his first thought in doing an interview was how he could transfer the important principles of truth from the successful coach to you. The great people of life understand that they are to be a bridge in life. Tom Mullins is the bridge between us and the coach that is successful.

I've known Tom for many years, and over the years I've watched him win with people. The reason is because he cares for others. That's what draws me to him, and that's what draws him to others. Many times people talk of Tom as a kind of pied piper leader; he walks in the room, empowers people, they join his team, and they're ready to follow him anywhere because they catch from him the spirit of "I want to help you be a winner."

My desire for you is to catch the Tom Mullins spirit from this book. As you read from page to page, you're going to feel it and know that Tom wants you to win. Read what he has to say and listen to the coaches, but don't just write down the principles; catch the spirit of a winner and pass it on to others. Don't make yourself a dead-end street. Share what you've learned from this book and add value to others by helping them to also play their best as they enter *The Leadership Game.*

Introduction
A New Model of Leadership

Tom, you've lost your teeth. Suck it up and get tough. Now, get back in there.
—COACH YOUNG, Lakota High School

When I was growing up in southern Ohio, sports, especially football, were at the center of my universe. My spirits rose each year with the advent of fall and the smell of freshly cut grass. I loved watching the game, I loved playing, and I idolized the men who taught me to play well.

My coaches demanded the very best of me at all times, taught me the balance of personal discipline and teamwork, and believed in me and helped me to believe in myself. They were not men of compromise; they would just as soon kick you in the pants as they would pat you on the helmet. Yet they made the game an adventure and winning a pure delight.

One Friday night when I was a sophomore, I went in to make a tackle, and the running back's face mask smashed through mine, breaking my nose and knocking out two front teeth. As I felt my way to my feet, someone noticed that I was the only kid with his back to the huddle and called a time-out to help me to the sidelines. One coach quickly surveyed the situation and stuffed cotton up my nostrils to stop the bleeding. "Tom," he said, peering into my mouth, "you've lost your teeth." He then reached through my mask and yanked out two more dangling by their nerve ends. He shoved more cotton into the spaces where four teeth had been, then slapped a new helmet on me, and said, "Son, suck it up and get tough. Now, get back in there." That was the first half.

I played the rest of the game with one eye swollen shut and cotton billowing from my nostrils, but I didn't quit, and my coach was proud. I was just a high school kid who didn't know much; but after that game I knew what resilience was, and I knew I could accomplish more than I thought I could. They are lessons I still use today.

When it was my turn to do the coaching, I intuitively modeled much of what I learned as a player, and I discovered that the principles were still effective. I took over a high school team with a long tradition of losing, and I taught the young men to win. We went undefeated in our second and third seasons and received the ranking of number one in the state.

I hung up my whistle after eight years coaching high school and seven in college football. Then I applied the same coaching principles to a small church I was asked to lead—after all, it was the only method of leadership I knew. It's now twenty-one years later, and we've grown from one hundred to more than twenty thousand ambassadors to the wonderful people in the our region of the country. The influence of our church today is exponentially greater than it was on that first Sunday—and coaching principles have a lot to do with it.

Leading Like a Coach

There are literally hundreds of books written on the general topic of leadership. I am not deterred, however, because there is a type of leadership that is powerful and reproducible that can transform an organization, a business, a church, or any other kind of group structure to become a highly effective, reliable, and self-sustaining entity in the marketplace of any society. I am referring to the leadership style of coaches—winning coaches.

In this book I have interviewed eight national championship football coaches (Bobby Bowden, Larry Coker, Phil Fulmer, Bill McCartney, Tom Osborne, Gene Stallings, Steve Spurrier, and Bob Stoops) and asked them what are their crucial leadership techniques that have led them to coach championship teams. Also, I have talked with businessmen and friends like Jack Nicklaus, A. L. Williams, and Bud Paxson and asked them about their leadership successes.

What did I find? Every one of these men agreed that there are certain patterns of leadership that are essential to develop winning teams—whether those teams play on the field, in corporate arenas, or in ministry circles. This book is my attempt to let the cat out of the bag—to tell leaders that they can learn from these coaches a new style of leadership that works. Period.

Since winning his twenty majors, Jack has constructed premier golf courses and stamped top products around the world with his legendary name. Bud is the creator and cofounder of the Home Shopping Network, and he founded PAX TV and Paxson Communications Corporation, the nation's largest broadcast television station group. Art was an original crusader of term life insurance, whose company, A. L. Williams, was the first in the industry to carry more than $300 billion in individual policies. These three clearly know how to lead, and they attribute their success in part to the principles they learned from coaching.

Jack used to come out to football practice when I coached his sons in high school. We'd spend time talking about life and family, the principles of coaching, and how he hoped his sons would learn lifelong lessons as he did. "I had relationships with my coaches," he explained. "Jack Grout was like another father to me. He taught me to think for myself. He taught me how to teach myself, how to be my own mentor. We'd go to the practice tee for three or four days and spend four or five hours each day, and he might mention golf once. But every time he saw something, he'd just say, 'Jack, let's see if we can keep your head behind the ball a little better.' That's all he'd say. He was fabulous."

Like Jack, Bud was an athlete who still applies the coaching principles he learned while excelling on the basketball court as a young man. A few weeks ago, he and I passed some time together discussing how the personal approach he learned from coaching helped him build one of the most successful organizations in America. "People are motivated by relationships," he explained, "and the fact that you take time to listen to their own personal story—their highs and lows—rather than just push them to do something. If they realize it's not always about the bottom line, but that you really have a genuine concern for them as a person, that's a huge motivating factor."

I also sat down with Art to ask how coaching helped him become one of the champions of term life insurance. His story is unique. He never intended to go into the insurance business. His dream was to be a high school football coach, and he followed it for seven years with great success, but his father's premature death positioned him to rethink his direction. With some counsel from family, he entered the insurance business, part time at first, until he found his niche in term life. From there he carved out his place in the industry's history by applying to his business approach the principles he learned from coaching. He explained this further.

Coaching taught me the little things that made the difference . . . Every day in business for twenty years, every day, I thought about some experience I had in coaching. Burning desire . . . incredible work ethic, mental toughness, the right attitude; I learned all those kinds of things from coaching.

Reflecting back on my years in business, another thing I learned is that many bosses in the business world look for these outside, artificial things like how you look and the kind of degrees you've got. But coaches learn that it's the inside things that make a difference. Coaches have a way of looking inside every person and seeing some good. They try to make you faster and stronger and tougher and make you feel good about yourself whether you're a third-string player or a first-string player. <u>Leaders have to understand that you get more out of people by praising them than you do by threatening them, because everybody wants to be somebody</u> . . . Nobody really wants a boss; everybody wants a coach because coaches have a way of making people feel special.

Art is right. Coaching principles are so effective because successful coaching requires a more personal approach to leading; this draws out more heartfelt responses from followers and more enduring results from teams. But as you will see, there is much more to coaching than that.

In the coming pages, we will discuss what I consider to be the top seven principles of effective coaching: (1) recruiting, (2) motivation, (3) momentum, (4) morale, (5) game planning, (6) game-day adjustments, and (7) celebration. I offer these thoughts in an effort not only to help you improve your current level of influence with your team, but also to help you better lead yourself.

> "Nobody really wants a boss; everybody wants a coach because coaches have a way of making people feel special."
> —ART WILLIAMS

I won't rely only on my thinking to tackle this task. While the seven coaching principles have served me well in more than three decades of leadership on and off the football field, I have also sought the opinions and advice of the eight championship coaches whose names I mentioned earlier. Some are friends to whom I've sent high school standouts, and all are undeniably successful leaders. Between these men there are eleven NCAA football national championships from 1990 to 2001:

Coach	School	National Championship(s)
Bill McCartney	Colorado	1990
Gene Stallings	Alabama	1992
Bobby Bowden	Florida State	1993, 1999
Tom Osborne	Nebraska	1994, 1995, 1997
Steve Spurrier	Florida	1996
Phil Fulmer	Tennessee	1998
Bob Stoops	Oklahoma	2000
Larry Coker	Miami	2001

Their candor and uncommon insight will help me present the seven coaching principles to you on a practical level so that you can immediately apply them to your leadership efforts.

Their teams' accomplishments are endorsement enough of the principles we will discuss, yet in our interviews I found that their smaller stories of success and failure on the road to their national championship seasons provide intriguing lessons that aren't found in most leadership books. In fact, I believe you will see within the coming pages a portrait of leadership you have not seen before; and it's my hope that it will change the way you view yourself, your people, and the challenges before you.

When I was a young coach at Georgetown College, our staff went to Columbus, Ohio, to visit with the legendary leader of the Buckeyes, Coach Woody Hayes. We sat in the staff meetings and watched the locker room procedures and even how the equipment managers passed out equipment. We observed how the trainers taped the athletes to prevent injuries. Then as we left the building and started toward the practice field, Coach Hayes leaned over to me and said, "Hey, son, come ride with me."

I might have learned more about leadership in that day than any other. And now I offer you a similar proposal. Come with me and ride alongside eight of the most successful coaches in collegiate football and learn what it really takes to lead yourself and your team to victory.

Section I

The Seven
Coaching Principles

1

Recruiting

The greatest recruiting coup happened when I was at Michigan . . . Anthony Carter scored fifty-nine touchdowns in high school on kickoff and punt returns. [He] was unbelievable. He was being recruited by Florida State, and Florida State, as you know, can throw the ball. I was representing Michigan, and we didn't throw the ball.
—COACH MCCARTNEY, University of Colorado
1990 National Champions

We thought we had Marshall Faulk coming to Nebraska. We had his English teacher, the principal, his mother—everybody around Marshall—about ten or twelve people, convinced he was coming to Nebraska. But right at the end he decided to go to San Diego State. What we found out was that Marshall wanted to be a running back.
—COACH OSBORNE, University of Nebraska
1994, 1995, and 1997 National Champions

My college coaching experience began at Georgetown College in Kentucky. It is a small Division II school, so I immediately accepted that recruiting a good team would require creativity and hard work. I remember one season I received a call from a coach in Lebanon, Ohio. He told me he had a good, solid tackle he wanted me to take a look at for next season. I was still trying to fill a few spots on my roster, so I drove to Lebanon to take a look at this kid named Jeff.

When I arrived at the school and observed the boy, I could see right away that he wasn't the prototypical big tackle I would jump at recruiting. He was only six feet one and weighed only 205 pounds.

He was too small for me to even consider offering a spot to, but I decided to go to his home anyway and see what happened.

I was surprised when I arrived at his parents' house and knocked on their door. His mother answered, and I was looking up at her. Then came his father to greet me, and I think his hand wrapped twice around mine. Before stepping into their house, I understood what Jeff's coach saw in him. Huge potential. I offered him a spot on the team.

When he showed up for summer practice a few months later, I didn't recognize him. He was six feet four and weighed 235 pounds. By the time he graduated, Jeff was six feet six, weighed 275 pounds, and had developed into a national All-American. More important, he helped turn the entire program around.

I was glad I knocked on Jeff's parents' door, and I learned two valuable lessons that day: one, you can't know someone's potential until you invest deeply in a recruiting process; and two, effective recruiting can significantly boost your chances for success.

How Deeply Are You Rooted?

Recruiting is the root system of your leadership. If your team is grounded with the hardy roots of top recruits, it can grow to the sky. On the other hand, if you're just plugging bodies into positions, your roots will remain shallow and weak, stunting your team's growth.

The ability to recruit top talent is fundamental for any successful team—most leaders understand that. In fact, any average leader can recognize good potential in players based on past and present performance. However, the ability to *convince* recruits to be part of a team is a different kind of challenge that only the best leaders do well. This process begins when you determine your recruiting edge.

The most elementary ingredient of good recruiting is a compelling vision for a recruit to embrace. In the business world, this vision is often grossly predictable: money now and more money later. The accompanying assumption is that the bigger the check, the more appealing the offer. Yet the best recruits are no longer buying into that notion.

Today's top recruits want something more than a big paycheck; they also want more than the promise of promotion. Paychecks and positions produce short-term enthusiasm, but they lack long-term appeal. If only money and status land you recruits, then more money and higher status will take them away. If you attract people to your team with something deeper, something more intrinsic, something linked to their sense of need and purpose and meaning, they will work harder and stay longer.

Does this mean that income shouldn't be part of your recruiting pitch if you're a corporate leader? No. But it does mean that the vision you communicate to recruits must find a place in their hearts as readily as their pockets.

College coaches know a lot about this subject. They do not have the luxury of a payroll, and the positions they offer aren't guaranteed. Neither money nor job stability is a viable promise. College coaches can offer only intangibles such as trust, hope, unity, possibility, and opportunity. However, such intangibles often promote commitment and loyalty better than anything else. That's because they are connected to something internal—they speak to an individual's sense of purpose and meaning—and this gives any leader a recruiting edge over the competition.

> The vision you communicate to recruits must find a place in their hearts as readily as their pockets.

What's Your Edge?

In my interviews with the national championship coaches, I asked what type of recruiting edge they possessed that set them apart from other top schools. Obviously the competition is fierce when it comes to wooing the best high school players in the nation each year, and these coaches have certainly proven their ability to get top talent on their teams. Here's how a few of the coaches accomplish this.

Coach Larry Coker of Miami said he recognizes that one of the biggest recruiting edges for his team is its tremendous football history. But other Florida universities—namely, Florida and Florida State—offer something similar.

"In our sales pitch, I think we really sell academics well," he told me.

> Football speaks for itself. Recruits have access to television or can pick up a *USA Today* . . . see a national trophy. All of that speaks for itself. The big thing is trying to make sure they realize that [Miami] is both football and an education. You look around the country—that school isn't out there that is better than us academically and football-wise. We [take] pride in [education] here . . . Just recently we had the top recruit in America committed to us—the best quarterback in the country. [The] main reason he wants to be here is because he loves the business school.

It would be easy for Coach Coker to rely on the school's winning tradition to entice recruits, but he understands that doesn't necessarily set Miami apart. The school's academic reputation does. The school considers itself the "Harvard of the South." To the recruit looking for a shot at a national championship *and* a top-notch education, Miami is certainly an excellent choice.

Looking back, Coach Tom Osborne admitted that Nebraska didn't have the same appeal that many top schools did. He therefore approached the recruiting process from a different angle:

We always felt recruiting was [about] the parents and . . . our campus because we didn't have beaches or mountains or a lot of social life . . . We tried to use a very personal approach. In fact, I would visit every player in his home. We didn't go on reputation or simply on what a coach told us about his player; we made sure we had done our homework.

Coach Osborne's edge found residence in the hearts of top recruits like Florida resident Tommy Frazier who liked the idea of belonging to a larger family. This edge did the team well as Frazier, according to Osborne, "put us over the hump from being a very good team to a great team" and catapulted the Cornhuskers to three national championships in four years.

It was tradition that drew recruits to Alabama during Coach Gene Stallings' reign. The great Bear Bryant once walked the very sidelines where the recruit stood, and it was an honor to be a part of Bryant's legacy. "I never tried to get a player to come to Alabama to play for me," Stallings confessed.

I wanted them to come to Alabama because of the rich tradition . . . When I was coaching for Coach Bryant, I definitely felt like it was to the young player's advantage to come to Alabama and play for [him] just to be around him, to listen to him, and to watch him because he's the only one that I know of that fits in that particular category.

Every good leader knows a good recruit when he sees one, but great leaders recognize and develop a recruiting edge that funnels the best recruits to their teams. This isn't automatic. Coach Coker admitted it is easy to count on Miami's recent trophy or even the vacation-like location to draw recruits, but neither may be enough. Championship-caliber players like Tommy Frazier will still sign with schools a thousand miles from their Florida homes if they have a better offer. The fact is that if you want to attract and sign the best people to your corporate team, you need to sharpen your recruiting edge, then use it to draw them in. Once you've determined what sets you and your company apart from the competition, you should take five steps to accomplish this.

Step 1: Communicate Your Vision in a Compelling and Concise Fashion.

In the days of leading his Huskers to three titles, Osborne recognized that knowing his recruiting edge was one thing; communicating it well was another. "We tried to make sure they had a good picture of what they would be going through for four years," he said, "because otherwise they could envision spending a lot of time on their social life with parties and girls when that isn't reality or what it's all about."

This clear picture is the foundation of your relationship with recruits. The vision you cast is your first opportunity to prove yourself trustworthy. Therefore, it is important for you not to overstate your case. "I think the big thing that I learned in the last twenty-seven years," admitted Coach Bobby Bowden of Florida State, "is that when you begin to build a program, you begin to build a reputation. When you talk to kids and say, 'Son, this is what I'm going to do,' well, he's [going to determine] whether 'this guy's a liar or this guy always does what he says he's going to do.' And so you establish a reputation. Finally, after twenty-seven years, most of these kids, their parents, and their coaches have a good idea of how we're going to run this program here."

The word picture you paint is about honesty more than persuasion. There is an element of your vision that says, "Here's who I am and here's who we are . . . and there's a place for you here if these things are appealing to you." Many leaders make the major mistake of trying to paint a utopian environment that any recruit would want to be part of—whether or not it is accurate. This is less risky and more widely appealing, so it seems. But the truth is that generalizations and idealizations set a leader up for failure.

"I always felt," stated Coach Steve Spurrier of Florida, "that honesty was the first fundamental key to recruiting." He understands that team members won't perform under the weight of an unfulfilled promise or an inflated assessment of reality. Eventually they will quit or become dead weight.

Coach Osborne stated,

> I think maybe one of the most important things was that when we recruited a player, I never promised him anything other than an opportunity. More recently, in the last part of my coaching career, the more common recruiting deception many coaches used was promising kids that they would start, that they would be given playing time, or that they would get to travel abroad. The problem is that those promises are very hard to keep—so you might recruit twenty players in a season and find that two years later you've got none of them left. This usually happens if you break trust with them and they find that you've lied to them. They're not going to play for you.

The foundation of your reputation is poured into the minds of recruits when you share your vision. If you are as candid as you are compelling, your team's foundation of trust will be steadfast for the long-term.

Step 2: Connect on a Personal Level.

Perhaps the most important step of recruiting is offering perceived value to your recruits. "In each home I went into," said Coach Bill McCartney of Colorado,

I would place a chair directly across from the kid. Then I would look right into that kid's eyes, but position myself where I could also turn and look at his parents. He and his parents would hear me tell him that I believed in him, that I needed him on my team, and that I had a place for him on my team . . . That guy has got to know the four most powerful words in the entire English language, which are, "I believe in you." When you communicate "I believe in you," you can recruit.

With this approach, McCartney pulled off what he calls his "greatest recruiting coup" when, as an assistant at Michigan under Bo Schembechler, he recruited a superstar away from his home state.

> "That guy has got to know the four most powerful words in the entire English language, which are, 'I believe in you.'"
> —BILL MCCARTNEY

"Anthony Carter scored fifty-nine touchdowns in high school on kickoff and punt returns," he recounted. "He was unbelievable. He was being recruited by Florida State, and Florida State—as you know—can throw the ball. I was representing Michigan, and we didn't throw the ball."

Coach Phil Fulmer of Tennessee concurred with McCartney's approach: "We learn not only about the recruit but what the recruit likes, who the recruit is dating, and who the key influencers are in the recruit's life. We go out and build relationships in this recruit's world so we know how to help that recruit understand that we care about him."

At the Division I level, where highly talented athletes typically have a number of options, recruiting on a personal level is of crucial importance. Jerry Rice is a good example of this. He was once asked in an interview why he chose to attend such a small college. He was an outstanding athlete in high school who set all kinds of records, and he went to Mississippi Valley State instead of one of the larger and more prominent universities. He replied that the Mississippi Valley State coach was the only one who came to his house and sat down with him and looked him straight in the face and said, "Jerry, I need you. I believe you will make the difference in our program." All the others wanted him to visit their campus, but that coach took time to meet him where he was—to connect with him on a personal level. It turned the team around.

Coach Osborne confessed a time when he was on the wrong side of the story:

> We thought we had Marshall Faulk coming to Nebraska. We had his English teacher, the principal, his mother—everybody around Marshall—about ten or twelve people, convinced he was coming to Nebraska. But right at the end he decided to go to San Diego State. What we found out was that Marshall wanted to be a running back. We and everybody else were recruiting him as a defensive back. If we had picked up on it, we would have had the best running offense in the country. I think Marshall Faulk would have set all kinds of records at Nebraska . . . We would have been happy to have him be a running back.

People have to buy into you before they'll buy into what you're offering, and they aren't likely to be sold if you're not engaging them enough to determine their values and desires. Sometimes we miss out on the Marshall Faulks because we don't go deep enough—we merely call references or former employers and assume we know the person, or at least assume he or she would make a great addition. The truth, however, is that until you really connect with an individual—real person to real person—encouraging him or her to join your team will be a more difficult task than it should be. Often it will be a futile task.

A two-way street. Beyond recruits' acceptance of your vision, a personal connection gives you a chance to determine the feasibility of their place on your team. Recruiting is really a two-way street: the recruit judging you and your vision, and you judging the recruit. Don't force a person onto your team because he reads well on paper. Confirm your findings. As a leader, you ought to recognize what sort of people your team needs before you begin recruiting. Connecting with an individual, then, is just your litmus test.

When I asked Coach Stallings about recruiting, he believed the most important aspect was being right about the person. "Typically," he explained, "the guy that everybody thinks is gonna make All-American fizzles. The guy nobody wants turns into a great player. So when somebody has a recruiting class, and they say, 'Boy it was a good one!' well, they don't know that is a good class any more than a goose."

In typical Stallings' fashion, the coach makes a good point. There are often conclusions we can't make about a person until he begins working and interacting with the other team members. This is an unavoidable risk in most situations. But there are ways to reduce the risk on the front end.

I believe recruits, at the very least, should pass the "Four C's" assessment in order to qualify for your team. You can make this assessment only if you spend quality time with them and ask lots of questions, then listen carefully. Based on the combination of what you already know about recruits and your evaluation of them at the time of your meeting, every individual should embody the following traits:

Character. You can verify aspects about a person's character by talking with the recruit and by interviewing important people in the recruit's life. You must do your best to determine on the front end what type of person you have so that you aren't burned down the road. Coach Bowden admitted, "I know people say that with all the trouble our kids get into, we must not look at character, but yes, we do. We look at it as hard as anybody else; but simply, kids just make mistakes." It's an important point.

The people you recruit will make mistakes—in fact, many will have made mistakes in their past that must be weighed with who they are today. However, past failure should never disqualify a recruit unless it was severe or has not been resolved. That's because past failure often makes a recruit a much stronger candidate for your team if he has grown from it. Bowden is good at discerning those who've learned from mistakes and those who are still prone to make them. Every leader will occasionally misjudge a recruit's character, but the best leaders see the obvious choices as well as the diamonds in the rough and know how to make them shine.

Competency. A major mistake that leaders tend to make is recruiting under pressure. We find a gaping hole that needs to be filled, and we settle for a paper champion. Having the position filled, we think, is better than its vacancy, so we flip through a file and pick the best read. It's rarely effective. Certainly it's more difficult and time-consuming to recruit the best, but long-term success depends on your having the best. Nothing hinders your potential more than high turnover, which makes it nearly impossible to sustain momentum and morale.

The key is to find competent people the first time—even if your search takes twice as long. And it's good to remember that the right recruit for you might not be tops on everyone else's list. Marshall Faulk wasn't even considered as a running back for any school but one—yet San Diego State took the time to discover his true talents, and the school was rewarded with one of the most electrifying backs in history.

Commitment. At Georgetown College, I would often take a less talented individual who was highly committed to excellence over a top recruit with his own agenda. If a recruit needed to wait for the right conditions to commit, I could generally predict that he would be a selfish player. But the recruit who was unconditionally committed was often a future star.

For example, I once recruited a young man out of Florida that no one else was interested in signing. He didn't have the size or speed that everyone was looking for, but I could sense that this guy was highly committed to excellence. He didn't have an outstanding freshman season with us, but he continued to work hard. He sought to learn every detail about his position in the defensive secondary. By his sophomore year Bruce took off and began to excel. He knew the tendencies of the top receivers he covered and was nearly flawless with the fundamentals. Because of this commitment, Bruce McNorton eventually went on to play for the Detroit Lions and enjoyed a successful career as a cornerback. If I had judged him on ability alone, I would have missed out on a major star.

Chemistry. There must be compatibility between recruits and existing team members in order to maintain team unity. You cannot succeed with a team full of selfish players who care only about their own accomplishments and accolades. Coach Coker agreed:

> I think that is a real challenge in talking to some of the coaches that have been here before. Many of them had great, talented teams that played at Miami without winning a championship. And when asked why they thought that was so, the words that came up were: "The guys became selfish." If you look at last year's [national championship] team, they were all-stars. We had a punter, a kicker, a center, a tight end, a quarterback, a running back, so you can just go down the list, and these are all national award candidates . . . [But we knew] if we were unselfish, we would have other opportunities, which is actually what happened. But each player has to buy into it. Sometimes they do and sometimes they don't. If you have quarterbacks that are there to win

Heisman Trophies, you may be good, but you will stumble somewhere along the way.

To contribute to the development of chemistry between recruits and the team, permit your current team leaders to be a part of the interviewing process, and allow their opinions to help shape your decisions. When the team leaders are excited about a recruit, they will have a stake in helping him be successful—this means greater efficiency for your team. Let's continue on this train of thinking as we discuss the third step in effective recruiting.

Step 3: Use a Team Approach.

Often, our teams are the best recruiters. "As much as anything, the players that are here sell the program," explained Coach Fulmer. "If we can get the recruits to the campus, then we've got a chance to sign them."

On my past teams, as well as in my present church, we cultivated an attitude of recruiting. Everyone on the team looks for ways to enhance the team, honing in on areas that still need support and regularly scouting to see if there are any recruits who might add something new and unique to our existing efforts. It should be the same for any team. Coach Coker summed it up well when he said, "Recruiting is a total team effort."

> Talent attracts talent, so your team should always assist you in recruiting.

Talent attracts talent, so your team should always assist you in recruiting. While it may not be the status quo, arrange for recruits to spend some time with their potential teammates. Your current team members may recognize characteristics about recruits that you may not. They may also be able to better convey the working environment and set accurate expectations. In addition, they can put a real face on the opportunity you are offering.

Don't underestimate the insight and inspiration that your current team members can offer. And certainly don't overlook the importance of maintaining the harmony of your team. When I asked Coach Osborne what set apart his three national championship teams from the others he'd coached, he said it was chemistry. He continued, "You certainly have to have a certain number of good athletes, but there are a lot of teams that have good athletes. You have to have good coaching, but there are a lot of teams that know X's and O's. I felt that the best teams that we had were teams that had a special bond. They were very close, made a fair amount of sacrifice, and had a willingness to forgo personal ambition for team goals."

The point is that you shouldn't surprise your team with a new member. This breeds awkwardness, and it shows little trust in the people you lead. By making recruiting a team effort, you convey an uncommon level of respect and trust. This will help you hire the best people and will deepen your influence with current followers. Your team will also be more willing to help the recruits succeed.

Step 4: Recruit Diversity.

Great coaches understand as well as anyone that every position is important. Take the kicker, for instance. He's in the sideline shadows for most of the game until, that is, the team is at the 40 and down by 2 points with only five seconds left on the clock. Then everyone's counting on him to be the hero. He's like that IT employee in a big corporation who nobody ever sees; he works in obscurity until someone can't access the eye-opening graph for that big presentation in thirty minutes. If you don't have a good kicker on the team or a savvy computer tech in the office in such situations, you're out of luck. The big kick is hooking to the left, and the big presentation has lost its hook. That's when poor leaders realize they should pay more attention to the people they hire.

In order to effectively recruit, you have to identify the specific talent that is necessary for your team's success. For example, the legendary coach Woody Hayes built his system on power football. This system was run out of an I-formation in the middle of the field. The center was the key man to his offense and the first man he recruited. The second man in line was his quarterback. The third man was his fullback. The fourth was his tailback. To run the I-formation effectively, he needed strength up the middle, so recruiting top talent in those four positions was vital to his team's success.

Leaders in any endeavor need to learn from this approach to team building. What type of system are you running? Where do you need self-starters and highly relational people and technical geniuses? Where do you need highly organized people? You need to know your answers, and you need to recruit them to your team, or change the way your team works.

Some leaders recruit people just like themselves. Although there's certainly nothing wrong with reproducing yourself, your team will be one-dimensional and move forward with a noticeable limp if this is all you do.

When I coached, it was easy to appreciate the diversity I had available to use within the team—I knew it made us better. What's interesting, however, is that when I started leading a church, I had a tendency to recruit people like me. I hired driven multitaskers who would get things done without asking a lot of questions. I plugged round holes that needed to be filled, but often with square and triangle pegs. As the church started to grow, I realized that a lot of work wasn't getting done properly, and we had no one qualified to do it well. I had to go back to the drawing board, which meant relying on new people's strengths instead of trying to shore up the existing team's weaknesses. I had to learn to lead in my strengths and recruit to my weaknesses.

Great leaders go about recruiting this way—the way a championship coach does. They come to terms with their teams' shortcomings and surround themselves with people who complement their weaknesses, not merely confirm their strengths. Above all, recruiting for diversity brings balance to a team, and balance is essential for long-term stability.

Step 5: Make Recruiting a Top Priority.

Let me wrap up our discussion of effective recruiting with this point: Recruiting doesn't just happen. You don't just hire good people, give them incentives to work hard, and end up with a fine-tuned team. That's the equivalent of pouring alphabet soup in a bowl and seeing "lucky you" appear in the broth.

Recruiting requires hard work. That may mean a bigger time commitment. That may take a greater investment of money. But let me ask you: Would you rather spend resources recruiting qualified people once or retraining unqualified people constantly?

That's the choice, really. Spend resources on the front end, and slowly but surely improve your team's effectiveness. Or spend resources fixing messes and never really get rolling.

If you think about it, recruiting is the first step toward momentum. Get the right people on the team, then figure out how to get them rolling at the same speed in the same direction. That's momentum in a nutshell—but there's a bridge between the right people and the right pace.

Once your team is ripe with top talent at key positions, you must then focus on maximizing that talent. That begins when you learn how to motivate your team members to perform at their highest level. Motivation gets momentum moving. This, too, is something college coaches know well.

2

Motivation

A friend of mine sent me a really beautiful walking stick. My
wife and I hike quite a bit, and the walking stick was carved
and was really pretty . . . I took it out to practice to show it
to some of the players, and they said, "Gosh, Coach, you
look like Moses." I'm thinking that Moses is this gray-
headed, bent-over, old guy, you know, so I gave the stick to
a manager and had him take it up to my office. Then that
night it hit me; Moses led the people to the promised land.
—COACH FULMER, University of Tennessee
1998 National Champions

When I moved to Florida to coach high school football, I
took over a team that had never experienced a winning season. The team won only four games the year before I arrived, and
there were only twenty players left on the team, so I faced an immediate test.

I went to work promoting the football program among the students and local folks. I spoke in churches and community centers trying to build the team. To my surprise, about one hundred players
showed up for summer ball.

I told them if they worked hard and remained committed, all of
them would dress for the games. I issued a no-cut policy. It wasn't
about their talent; it was about rewarding their desire and their hearts
to make a difference together.

When it was time to hand out equipment, I lined up the former
players first and then those who looked as if they had good potential.
The final player to come through the line at the end of that very long

day was a young man by the name of Carl Pierce. He was built like a No. 2 pencil. When he stepped forward, I asked him what position he wanted to play. "I want to be a wide receiver, Coach," he asserted. I called into the equipment room, "Hey, guys, do we have any wide receiver pads left?" "No, Coach," they called back. "We only have one pair of shoulder pads left." We'd already gone through all the varsity, junior varsity, and ninth grade equipment, trying to suit up all these kids. "Okay," I said, "just bring them out anyway. We'll make them work."

When I saw the shoulder pads, I immediately recognized who had worn them last—a defensive tackle who weighed about three hundred pounds. I put the pads on Carl, and they nearly fell down over his shoulders. He actually stuck his arm up through the neck hole. "Coach," he said, "I think these are too big." "No, son," I replied. "Here's the deal. You have freedom in these pads. You can move around and won't be restricted at all—and you'll be able to catch that ball from any position." In truth, I could have twirled the pads around his neck like a propeller.

I then asked him what size helmet he needed. "A 6?" he said. When I asked the equipment guys if they had any small helmets, they called back, "No, Coach, we only have one helmet left." "Well," I said, "bring it out. We'll make it work." It was the helmet that fit that three-hundred-pound lineman—an 8¾. We stuffed that thing with double cheek pads and any other kind of padding we could find, but we still couldn't get it to fit right. No matter how hard we padded it up and strapped it down, it slid all over Carl's face when he started jogging. (One time I saw him running out to practice, and his nose was sticking out the ear hole.)

And of course, we had only one pair of pants left. Carl could fit both legs down one leg of the pants. We were out of belts, so he had to use shoe strings to keep the pants up. We finally got him suited, but he was a pretty sad sight.

When he ran out on the field, the other players laughed. He couldn't do much except hold onto his pants with one hand and steady his helmet with the other. Yet Carl Pierce had something fierce inside him, and he kept coming out to play.

When it was time for the first game, I had to let him dress because I made a promise to the team. I hate to admit it, but I hid him between a couple of big players so he wouldn't embarrass us when we took the field.

Our team made strides that year, and we won our first four games. One more win would set a new school record. During the fifth game we were trailing late and scored a touchdown that put us in the lead. All we had to do was kick the ball off, hold them for one defensive series, and let the clock run out. We would have five wins for the first time in school history.

As the team prepared to kick off, I counted only ten players on the field. I turned around and looked at my assistant coach and growled, "Get somebody on the field!" He turned and grabbed the first player standing next to him and threw him onto the field. It was Carl. I started screaming to stop the play. I gave a time-out signal to the official, and he told me we had no more time-outs left.

Carl didn't even know how to line up. He didn't know any of the kickoff formations. Somehow he ended up in the contain position on the outside—one of the most crucial positions on the kickoff team. I glared at my assistant coach, and if looks could kill, he'd be dead today.

The official blew the whistle for the kickoff, and Carl took off running down the field. Pads and body parts were flapping everywhere. Then there was a huge collision at the 25-yard line, and our guys started screaming, "Fumble! Fumble!" They jumped up and started pointing and shouting, "We've got the ball! We've got the ball!" Our sideline erupted, knowing we had won the game.

And then, from the bottom of the pile, emerged the hero. Sprinting to the sidelines, hugging the ball in his arms, Carl was yelling, "I got the ball, Coach! I got the ball!"

When we reviewed the game film the next morning, we saw him sprinting down the field, holding onto his pants, while his shoulder pads and helmet flopped up and down—he looked like a bobble-head doll. Then the boy returning the ball veered right into Carl. He let go of his pants and slammed into the boy, knocking the ball loose. Somebody then speared Carl in the back and knocked him onto the ball.

On Monday morning I got him out of class and took him down to the sporting goods store to buy him some equipment that fit. I had to go to the junior department to do it, but we got him everything he needed. When I asked if there was anything else he wanted, he said, "Coach, I want some forearm pads because I want to be a special teams specialist. I want to go down and hit people!"

When he came out to practice later that day, the players cheered for him. They knew how hard they had been on Carl. He accepted their cheers graciously because he had a desire in his heart to be a part of a team—despite the obstacles—and the team realized it was better for it.

I put Carl on the kickoff team for the next game because I wanted to honor him for his great effort. Wouldn't you know it—he was in on the tackle. I never took him off the special teams after that, and at the end of the season his teammates voted him the Most Improved Player. The next year they voted him captain of the special teams.

Motivation Maximizes Talent

You and I can learn a lot from Carl. His story demonstrates the sheer power of motivation to elevate common talent to an uncommon level. His body wasn't big enough, but his heart was—and that made his ability bigger than his body.

Motivation is often the only difference between the winner and the loser. This is no more evident than when two great football teams are doing battle. Sure, there are breaks and mistakes on both sides of the ball, but those can be overcome. Almost without fail, the team that ends up on top when both teams are equally talented is the team that wanted the win more than the other.

We are privy to examples every year when one team routs the same team that beat it by 3 points earlier in the year. Call the motive revenge or payback or retribution, it's still the result of one team that wants to win against one team that *will not* lose. It's the power of motivation, and a leader must learn to harness it to maximize a team's talent.

No leader understands the power of motivation better than football coaches whose players are not paid to win. The vast majority of high school and college players have no incentive to excel but for the thrill of victory and the satisfaction of accomplishment. Their motives are simple; yet maximizing them is no simple task.

Championship coaches like Bill McCartney have a unique capacity to move a player's motives to action so that he performs at his very best. I asked him about his thoughts on motivation, and he shared, "Morale is to the physical as four is to one. Your attitude is four times as important as your actual physical abilities." He went on to describe how a highly motivated athlete can outper-

> "Morale is to the physical as four is to one."
> —Bill McCartney

form a more physically gifted athlete in any game. It makes sense then that the greatest leaders don't necessarily have all the greatest players. The greatest leaders know how to get the best out of every player, in every situation, which in turn produces a highly effective team. There are six keys to accomplishing this:

Key 1: Be Self-Motivated.

When I asked Coach Bowden about motivation, he described the forming of his philosophy this way:

> When I first came up in coaching, fifty-something years ago, I often heard, "Don't do as I do; do as I say." I was kind of raised on that philosophy. If Coach wants to go out and get drunk, he can do it—but don't you do it. [But] I don't go with that philosophy. I go with the philosophy that I'm not going to ask the kids to do anything that I wouldn't do. I'm not going to ask them *not* to do it if I'm going to go do it. So I recommend that you keep your credibility. Don't tell a kid not to do something if you're going to go do it. Set an example.

As a leader, you have to understand that the spark of enthusiasm starts with you. You hold the match and your team holds the torch. Before your team gets fired up, you have to light the match. Only then can you light its torch.

Many leaders make the mistake of passing the proverbial torch to their teams, then waiting in expectation for the flames and smoke. The flames rarely appear, because that's not leadership; that's dictatorship. Forgive me for stating the obvious, but leadership requires you to lead—to set an example to follow. If you're just barking orders, don't expect your people to be highly motivated. Expect them to be fearful, resentful, or lethargic.

When I think about what first motivated me as a young player, I'm reminded of my best coaches' enthusiasm for the game. Their passion was evident in everything they said and did. They stayed late after practice to work with players who needed help. It was clear they took interest in helping us meet our goals. I pushed harder and faster and longer because I wanted to exceed their expectations. They gave me their full effort; therefore, they deserved my full effort. In fact, back then I believe I thought less about winning than I did about performing my very best. That made me a winner through and through.

Without enthusiasm at the top, team members can, at best, motivate themselves. There are always people on our teams for whom this is easy, but they are rare. My experience is that most people not only want but need their leader to be excited about the direction they are headed. When the leader is self-motivated, the people follow suit. Put a pendulum clock in your office to remind you of this truth.

One night in 1656, as the clock's inventor lay in bed, he noticed something odd across the room. The pendulums on his clocks were swinging in unison, even though he knew with certainty they hadn't begun this way. Many experiments ensued, and what the Dutch scientist Christiaan Huygens later discovered was that the largest clock with the strongest rhythm pulled the other pendulums into sync with itself. Its pace dictated the others' pace. Scientists named this physical phenomenon "entrainment," and it has since become evident throughout nature . . . and, I might add, leadership.

Key 2: Invite Them into a Bigger Story.

Each of us wants to be part of something bigger than ourselves. Call it a purpose or a destiny or simply a desire to get past all the insufficiencies of our current existence, an individual's yearning to reach beyond his limitations is a seed of greatness waiting for a stream of motivation.

Carving a path to that seed in your followers' hearts is a simpler task if there is a story being told. Coach Fulmer told me how he accomplished this:

A friend of mine sent me a really beautiful walking stick. My wife and I hike quite a bit, and it was carved and was really pretty. It showed up at school about the time I was walking out to practice . . . I took it out to practice to show it to some of the players, and they said, "Gosh, Coach, you look like Moses." I'm thinking that Moses is this gray-headed, bent-over, old guy, you know, so I gave the stick to a manager and had him take it up to my office. Then that night it hit me; Moses led the people to the promised land.

The next day, I put the team in a circle . . . I said, "Okay, yesterday you guys said that I looked like Moses." And I reminded them that Moses led the people to the promised land and that this stick was going be the focal point of our energy. So it became our "synergy stick." I told them that they couldn't tell their girlfriends, their parents, or the media. It was just between us. But every time they saw the stick on the field they were to think about that meeting and what it would take to win the national championship. I gave it to Al Wilson, who was our team captain and leader, and he took it to the meetings and to the practice field. And the next day we gave it to Mercedes Hamilton, an offensive lineman, who was one of the captains.

They really bought into it . . . We'd get on the plane to go on a trip, and they'd say, "Hey, Coach, got the stick?" It was always on the sidelines, and you know, it was one of those unique things that really struck home.

A trip to the promised land wasn't just an inspiring story; it was Coach Fulmer's way of inviting the young men on his team into an epic of their own. The walking stick wasn't the source of their motivation; it was a constant reminder of the larger story they were writing every day in every practice and every game. That year, 1998, Tennessee's story was complete when the team crossed over to the NCAA version of the promised land by winning the national championship.

The key to inviting your team into a bigger story is that it must be *the team's* story. Many leaders make the mistake of filling the minds of their followers with tales of team victory that result only in personal recognition. A good story has a narrator, yes. And that is your place as a leader. But you can tell the story only the best that you can foresee it; this is your vision. However, you cannot write the story. The pen is in the hands of your people. This is why it is critical that they understand their part. Whether you use a prop like the synergy stick or a story like Moses and the promised land to introduce your team members to their epic, the goal is to invite them into a story they will want to be a part of, and then let them begin writing while you act as the editor and narrator.

Key 3: Let the Team Help Determine the Plot.

Hand in hand with the bigger story is the plot. If the story is the vision you invite your team into, then the plot of the story is the goals required to carry out the vision. And the team must be involved, because the players are the story's composers.

One of the things unique to Nebraska during the days of Coach Osborne's reign was his willingness to involve the teams in goal setting. He explained,

> So often a coach comes in and says, "Our goal is to do this and this and this . . . ," and that's all well and good, but then it's the coach's goals, not the players'. So we would say, "You twenty players write down your top five goals for the season in order of importance to you." Then we would incorporate those with ours and . . . we would put them up. Usually they would list a national championship and an undefeated season. Then we would say, "Okay, these are your goals. Now how are we going to get there?"

Coach Osborne motivated his team because he trusted the players with the script to their own story. As the leader, he prodded them in the right direction, much like an editor fine-tunes a writer's story line. Once this transfer of ownership occurred, Osborne primarily acted as the narrator of his championship teams' stories, reminding them of what had happened, telling them what was happening, and foreshadowing what would happen if they held to the goals that made up their plot. That was all the motivation they needed.

Coach Stoops described his role as a motivator in similar fashion: "[My job] is constantly keeping their eyes on their goals and how to achieve them." When the leader offers a compelling story and then transfers ownership of the plot to his team, a higher level of responsibility ensues. This unifies the players' hearts and minds on the goals necessary to live out their epic. More than that, it motivates them to follow through.

Coach McCartney explained it this way: "You have to first show a man the prize; then he'll pay the price. If you can *keep* his eyes on the prize, he'll pay a *great* price. There are three things about showing them the prize: you have to see it clearly, you have to show it creatively, and you have to say it constantly. As you do those three things, you'll get everybody to take their eyes off themselves and the pain they're in, and they'll start to pay a great price for the prize."

Key 4: Reward Your Team Members Individually.

Although he is probably not voicing it, every follower is asking, *How am I valuable to the team?* As the leader, you have the job of making sure each team member knows his answer. Coach Spurrier explained his philosophy at Florida:

One part of coaching that I really believe in is making every player feel important. Not just your star players, but even your practice players should feel important. Obviously, at Florida, with over a hundred players on the team, you've got forty or fifty that very seldom get to play in the real game. So you need to make those players feel important and that they are contributing to the success of the team . . . Then when you win a championship, every player on the team shares in it.

When a leader can pinpoint each team member's value, the leader is able to reward him individually and, when appropriate, praise him publicly. The leader reminds each team member that he is valuable and has a stake in the team's victories.

As a leader, you must learn to recognize and celebrate the small successes surrounding the bigger victories. These bind teammates to each other and motivate them toward the greater success of the team. We'll discuss this further in Chapter 4 when the coaches talk about team spirit.

Key 5: Let Team Members Hold Each Other Accountable.

It's one thing for a coach to pump up his team with a fiery pep talk in the locker room; it's another to fire up the players when they're on the field. Most good leaders face a similar challenge. They can readily motivate their team to *want* to act, but they cannot act for the members or walk by their sides every step of the way. Often, this is something only another teammate can do.

A coach might have his team breaking down the locker room walls before the game, but when the other team returns the opening kickoff for a touchdown, the main thing keeping the players motivated is each other. When they look each other in the eye, their enthusiasm is either held back or drawn out. A great leader knows how to keep his players high on each other.

I learned this early in my coaching career, really, by accident. As a high school coach, I was always looking for new ways to motivate our team. One time we were scheduled to play Sun Coast High School, where Anthony Carter attended. The year before I arrived, his team beat us 63-0. Knowing my team would need something extra for motivation, I wrote "Sun Coast High School 63" in big letters and a small "Palm Beach Gardens 0" on a white bed sheet and hung it in the locker room the week leading up to the game. My plan was to rip the sheet off the wall before the game, tear it to shreds, and then send our team out to tear Sun Coast to shreds on the field.

I thought it might be difficult to rip a bed sheet, so I frayed the edges in advance to make it easier, but when I grabbed it off the wall in that moment of excitement, I had folded the corner over so I couldn't tear it. I yanked and jerked on the thing, but it wouldn't budge. I tried biting it, but even that didn't work. Eventually I just stood there paralyzed—my motivating moment dying in front of me.

Then suddenly one of the smaller players on our team, Mark Cristaldi, got up from the back of the room and came charging at me. He grabbed the bed sheet and began ripping it with his teeth. He tore it into pieces, tossing them around. The team jumped in and began throwing the pieces in the air and shredding every last inch. Next thing I knew, they were howling in a war cry together, and each of them had a piece of the sheet tied to his helmet, shoved into his pants, or held in his hand, waving it in the air, when we took the field.

Later in the game I called for one of my players and said, "Come here, son. I want you to go in." He said, "Coach, I can't go in. I don't have a piece of the thing." I said, "Piece of the *thing?* What thing?" He said, "You know, a piece of the thing we tore up in the locker room." I walked over to a kid who had a piece hanging off his face mask. I jerked it off and handed it to the other kid and said, "Now, get in the game!"

We won the game—and it wasn't because I had motivated them well in the locker room. It was because Mark Cristaldi stepped out and put himself on the line. When he did that, the team members rallied around each other—something I couldn't accomplish on my own.

Enthusiasm is contagious. That's why, without fail, the best way to keep your team motivated is to let members feed off each other. There is much you can do and say on the front end to inspire them, but once they're in the thick of things, the faces they see most are each other's. If you can teach your team to hold each other up in good and bad times, your capacity to motivate the members will be vastly expanded.

Key 6: Deserve to Win.

Nothing builds confidence more than old-fashioned hard work. I learned this lesson the hard way in my first season as the coach of Palm Beach Gardens High. Skinny Carl's fumble recovery had just helped us win our fifth game of the season, an all-time high for the school, and our next opponent hailed from Fort Pierce Central High. The team was number one in the state and the defending state champion. It was also undefeated and loaded with talent. Eddie Edwards, who eventually played for the Cincinnati Bengals, was a defensive tackle, and Don Lattimer, who went on to play for the Denver Broncos, was a linebacker. I mean, that team was loaded for sure. We were 5-0 at the time, so we were fired up to take on Fort Pierce Central and dethrone them. We went out and played hard.

During the last minute of the game, they threw a touchdown pass over our safety's head, who mistimed his jump. He went up a little too early, and his hang time wasn't enough. The ball just cleared his hands. The receiver caught it and ran for a touchdown and won the game.

When Fort Pierce Central left the field, those guys did something that just ripped me to the core. They jogged off chanting, "We won because we worked harder! We won because we worked harder!"

In the locker room, I told my team that would never happen again. No team would *ever* beat us because we hadn't worked hard enough. I called a practice that night.

The next year we took the field against Fort Pierce Central. Once again, the team was the defending state champion, undefeated, and ranked number one in the state for the 4A division, the highest at that time. We were number one in the state for the 3A division, and we were also undefeated.

We traveled to their field to play for their homecoming, and the place was packed. Before we took the field, I said, "Gentlemen, you *will* win this game because you are *prepared* to win this game." We scouted that team to the extent that we even knew the names of the girlfriends of the players. We had worked our butts off.

That night we took the field and stuck it to 'em. We beat them 39-6! Then afterward our guys left the field chanting, "We won because we worked harder! We won because we worked harder!"

There's no doubt hard work builds a team's confidence. And confidence is the key to motivation no matter what field you're taking. Coach Coker aptly summed up the goal of motivational leadership when he told me, "I like the phrase, 'Deserve to win.'"

One of Coach Spurrier's motivational philosophies at Florida was daily improvement. This hinged on a habit of hard work that constantly raised his teams' confidence. "My basic way of motivating was more of a persistent level of trying to be your best," he said.

> We tried to practice well each day, and we tried to approach every day very similarly. We tried to improve as a season progressed . . . [The team knew] we should play a little bit better than last week no matter who the opponent is. I'm a big believer that, like Coach Wooden, we try to get ourselves ready to play, whether or not we knew the other team . . . or who their best players were or their type of defense . . . things like that. We concerned *ourselves* with trying to play the best we could each game.

I had a friend tell me that one reason I won so many games at Florida was because we very seldom got upset by those teams that weren't in the top twenty-five. I think we lost only one in twelve years . . . We generally beat the teams we were supposed to, and I think that was because we prepared to play the best we could just as we would when we played Tennessee, Georgia, Florida State, and so forth.

More than once in our interview, Coach Spurrier referenced the influence of Coach Wooden, the legendary UCLA basketball coach who admittedly never scouted an opponent. Instead, his practices focused on mastering the fundamentals required of each team member, which gave each young man the confidence in his ability to perform. As it so happened, that was Wooden's catalyst for leading his UCLA teams to ten national championships in twelve years, a feat unmatched in the history of sports.

Ultimately the most important aspect of motivation is its capacity to build a team's confidence. This is your primary role as the motivator. Empty promises and pipe dreams leave a follower reluctant to believe in the leader's ability to lead and, far worse, in his own ability to perform. If you've ever felt that your team was in a slump, this is most likely the cause. Low self-confidence leaves a team lethargic and lazy. But when a leader leads from a place of honesty and integrity and employs creative motivational strategies like those we've discussed, both confidence and character are elevated. And a team brimming with confidence rolls over the competition. The key to continual victory is maintaining that confidence; we call the result momentum.

3

Momentum

In 1958, Bear Bryant left Texas A&M and came to the University of Alabama and had a complete rebuilding job to do there. One year later, in 1959, I was appointed the head football coach at Sanford University, which is in Birmingham and only forty-five miles away. I was able to watch how he brought the Alabama program along. I think he won his first national championship in '61. Before he left, I think he had won about five.

—Coach Bowden, Florida State University
1993 and 1999 National Champions

We prepared the same way every week. We had the same rhythm. Even if we were a fifty-point favorite, it didn't make any difference; we still prepared the same, and as a result, we seldom got upset by somebody we should have beaten.

—Coach Osborne, University of Nebraska
1994, 1995, and 1997 National Champions

B ud Wilkinson," Coach McCartney explained, "was the last one to win forty-seven in a row . . . Eddie Crowder, who played quarterback at Oklahoma [under Wilkinson], told me that on Sunday nights Bud would go in by himself and look at film of the next opponent until he was convinced that there was no way that Oklahoma could win unless they played a perfect game. When he came out of there, you couldn't be around him unless you were going to go after it with all your heart . . . Whenever a kid's thinking like that, he knows he can't take a play off because every play can make the difference in a game. Somehow, some way, you've got to be able to get them to see the next game as far more important than the last game."

Coach McCartney was talking to me about momentum, the invisible force that seems to carry great teams to victory after victory. He attributed his teams' ability to create momentum to the influence of Bud Wilkinson, the legendary Oklahoma coach who is credited with the longest winning streak in NCAA history.

"Records didn't interest him," writes Bob Carter of ESPN.com,

nor did polls, predictions or other superficial methods of evaluating success. Bud Wilkinson valued the kind of people who played football for him and what they learned about discipline, readiness and character . . . Granted, Wilkinson won football games—more in one stretch than any major-college coach in history. His Oklahoma teams set the NCAA record by winning 47 consecutive games. But first and foremost, he wanted his players to understand the importance of being prepared. "If you have the will to prepare," Wilkinson said, "things will usually work out quite well, and the will to win will take care of itself."[1]

Preparation Precedes Momentum

This thread of preparation wasn't unique to Coach McCartney's insights on momentum. Coach Bowden applied a similar philosophy early in his career. He explained,

I came up under coaches like Frank Thomas . . . Bobby Dodd, Willy Butts, Bud Wilkinson. Those were the guys that were kind of famous as I was getting into coaching. But in 1958, Bear Bryant left Texas A&M and came to the University of Alabama and had a complete rebuilding job to do there. One year later, in

1959, I was appointed the head football coach at Sanford University, which is in Birmingham and only forty-five miles away. I was able to watch how he brought the Alabama program along. I think he won his first national championship in '61. Before he left, I think he had won about five. I was [at Sanford] for four years and was able to meet and listen to him and talk to all his coaches. I would go down there often to watch him do spring training. That period of four years was probably more influential on my coaching than any other period of the fifty years I've been in it . . . The thing I learned from him that he always stressed was to have a plan for everything. That's what I've tried to do at Florida State.

If anyone knows about effective leadership, it's Coach Bowden, who, on October 25, 2003, led Florida State to victory over Wake Forest. He became the winningest collegiate coach in history. This alone gives testimony to his ability to lead. But what may be most remarkable about his leadership is his teams' unrivaled capacity to sustain momentous streaks.

Are You a Streaker?

Under Bowden's preparation-centered leadership, Florida State set NCAA records by playing in twenty-two consecutive bowl games, receiving fourteen consecutive top-five rankings, and in 1999, the year of its second national championship, by becoming the first team in college football history to remain the Associated Press No. 1 for an entire season.[2] That's real momentum, and Bowden's teams' streaks suggest that it may not be as magical as some think.

As leaders, we may too easily fall prey to the assumption that momentum just happens, and when it does, we have the job of trying to lasso it and hold onto it as long as we can. But that's a lazy conclusion. Sure, our teams will have breaks from time to time, and those breaks will make it easier for us to accomplish goals; but no leader can wait on good fortune and maintain a high degree of success. Only a Florida fan would imply that Florida State's momentum over the years was lucky.

You've probably heard it said that the most successful people "make their own luck." It's another way of saying that the most successful people don't wait for something good to happen; by being prepared, they *make* it happen again and again. This perpetuates momentum.

By the way, Coach Bowden didn't inherit a great team when he took over Florida State; the team had won only a total of four games in the three years before he arrived.[3] His team's momentum was not good fortune; it was earned with preparation-centered leadership.

When teams like Florida State are well-prepared, momentum killers are minimized, and momentum keepers are maximized. In other words, the team is less fazed by mistakes and more equipped to exploit successes. But there is more to momentum than creating it during the course of one endeavor.

To keep success rolling, a leader must guide his team to sustain momentum over the course of an entire season. This is where preparation meets focus, and no leader knows it better than a college coach who faces a new test every week.

His weekly challenge is not merely an abstract goal like bettering customer service or working together more effectively; for a championship-level coach, the team's weekly challenge is do or die. One loss and a team's championship hopes are severely dampened—and usually dashed altogether. Over the twelve-year span from 1990 to 2001 (excluding the 1991 season), only three of the interviewed coaches won the national championship with one loss during the season. Take a look at the teams' records at the end of each year:

National Championship	School	Record
1990	Colorado	11-1
1992	Alabama	13-0
1993	Florida State	12-1
1994	Nebraska	13-0
1995	Nebraska	12-0
1996	Florida	12-1
1997	Nebraska	13-0
1998	Tennessee	13-0
1999	Florida State	12-1
2000	Oklahoma	13-0
2001	Miami	12-0

In fact, since 1869, when Princeton was proclaimed the champion with a 1-1 record, only twenty-three national champions lost a game during the season. Only once, in 1960, did a national champion have two losses—Minnesota was 8-2 to finish the season and was proclaimed champion by the Associated Press, the United Press International, and the National Football Foundation and Hall of Fame.[4]

The point is that there is little room for loss of momentum in the career of a championship leader. To keep hopes alive, he must not lose a game. His team must be well-prepared to meet each goal, and the team must become more effective and efficient as the season progresses and the challenges become more difficult. There's a reason why many teams schedule easier games early in the season—their coaches understand that the best way to take on their toughest challenges is to already have a big head of steam rising.

Sustaining Momentum with Singular Focus

When it comes to creating momentum, a coach's job begins with relevant and thorough preparation, but preparation alone does not sustain momentum from week to week. That's because a team's challenges change—in college football, they change dramatically. While the overall goal of victory stays the same, the steps to get there are progressive, and a team's preparation must follow suit. Coach Stallings explained it this way: "I didn't ever look beyond the game that we were playing that particular week. That game required all of our attention."

Once your team is well-prepared to see the big vision, it's easy to look beyond the steps necessary to get there. It's what we call in football "looking past your opponent," and it has led to the downfall of many would-be champions.

A paradox of leadership is that it's your job to help your team envision the big goal, and it's also your job to keep the team focused on the next step—in essence to help the members remember the main goal and forget it at the same time. This is why momentum is such a challenge. College coaches have a necessary progression of steps that they *must* take if they are to meet their overall goal of a national championship: they must win every game, one at a time. For most leaders, the motivation to succeed is not as inflexible, but every leader can certainly create the same level of focus and expectation.

Four common actions surfaced when I asked the eight coaches about meeting the challenge of sustaining momentum throughout a season. Their actions represent four lessons that every leader should teach the team in order to sustain momentum for the long haul.

Lesson 1: Teach Them That Every Play Counts.

Have you ever seen a football team "lose" for three and a half quarters of a game, then pull out a win in the end? When it happens, we're tempted to say things like, "They were lucky," or "The other team beat themselves," but the truth is usually more tangible than that.

Don't the best teams, the championship teams, find a way to win no matter how the game looks on a stat sheet? Often, the winning records of championship teams are not without ugly wins and *near* losses; but the win column doesn't discriminate between near losses and blowouts. A win is still a win no matter how it looks or how it comes about—even if it's seized in the final minutes.

Consistently successful coaches understand that training their players to give their all on every play—even when they're down by two scores with only three minutes left in the game, or they're faced with a huge obstacle—is the key to unwavering confidence and consistent victory. One way I accomplished this as a coach was by convincing my teams that we were better conditioned than our opponents; therefore, the longer the game went on, the more equipped we were to play better.

Coach Spurrier's similar approach to sustaining momentum was stressing persistence and the importance of getting better as the game progressed. "Each player," he said, "does not know when he might be the difference maker in the game." When you can convince your team members of this truth, they will be prepared to make big plays, and they will never feel that victory is out of reach. When every team member is constantly asking, "Will this be the big play?" your team will rarely miss a golden opportunity to finish strong or to turn defeat into victory.

This lesson cannot be taught in the final minutes before taking the field; it must be promoted in the trenches of day-to-day preparation. My coaches taught me this as I came up through high school. On every play, in every practice, and in every game, give your all. When I made the team at Georgetown College, I applied the same lesson, and it won me a very important friendship.

Ernie Tackett was from the hills of Kentucky. He was our center, and he had such thick calluses on his feet from running through those hills that he wore those old-fashioned high-top cleats without socks. This guy was pure country and as tough and mean as they come.

We were practicing some extra points one day, and the coaches called a bunch of us freshmen over and said, "Just kind of rush 'em and put some pressure on 'em while they're practicing." So I got down there all gung ho, trying to prove myself to the team. On the snap of the ball, I went charging through the line between Ernie and the guard, and I blocked the kick. The coach jumped all over Ernie, just ripped him up one side and down the other. Ernie came back to the line and told me, "You try that again, and I'm gonna knock your head off."

That only made me want to try harder, so on the next snap I tried charging through again and got tripped up and landed at the bottom of a big pile. When Ernie got up, I was still at the bottom waiting for the rest of the guys to get off. He noticed me lying there and turned around and kicked me in the side of my helmet. He hit me so hard with those huge high-tops, I was seeing stars. Nevertheless, I popped up, furious, and charged him while he was in the huddle with his head down. I grabbed his big body and yanked him to the ground, then pounded him with everything I had. Next thing I knew, I felt this powerful surge. He picked me up like a bale of hay and threw me off him. I popped to my feet again, and he was already coming at me.

Those days they let players fight out their frustrations—it was

Those days they let players fight out their frustrations—it was their way of separating the men from the boys. Fortunately ours was the only fight the coaches ever broke up. I'm certain it saved my life.

their way of separating the men from the boys. Fortunately ours was the only fight the coaches ever broke up. I'm certain it saved my life.

After practice, Ernie still hadn't forgotten. He told me he was gonna get me. I was standing in the freshmen locker room, and suddenly he and his big shoes were at the door. "Where's Mullins?" he shouted. Everybody froze. It was like high noon in Dodge City—someone was about to die, and everyone knew it wasn't Ernie. I turned around to show my face and grabbed my helmet by the mask; I was gonna use it as a club to defend myself from this big, mean, hairy guy.

"What do you want, Tackett?"

"Good practice, Mullins," he replied and then turned around and walked out. To the surprise of everyone, including me, I earned his respect by taking every play seriously and working hard. He knew it made us better as a team. Ernie and I became good friends after that day—I made sure of it.

Lesson 2: Teach Them to Appreciate One Victory at a Time.

Not only do leaders need to keep their teams focused on every play, they must help them see the importance of every game. This challenge resonates with every championship coach whose team is often favored to win.

When I asked Coach Bob Stoops of Oklahoma how his Sooners upheld their momentum as a perennial contender, his answer was succinct, almost matter-of-fact: "You focus and isolate individually from week to week. Everyone talks about [preparing for one team at a time], and the media tries to say it's cliché, but it isn't. The really good teams are focused on *one* game."

Coach Coker agreed:

> Focus on the job at hand because a lot of distractions come up. For example, in this interview we are talking about winning streaks; we are talking about repeat; we are talking about all these things that

have nothing to do with practice today. So I think the main thing [for sustaining momentum] is saying, "Let's focus on what is really important, what we really have control of." We don't have control over the national championship game. Now, if we win the rest of these games and we get [there], that is a different story. But the only thing we have control over and should be concerned about is: How well did we practice today?

Ironically, focusing on one game at a time is sometimes more difficult when a team's confidence is high. The players can see the finish line, and getting ahead of themselves can be easy. Unless a leader can keep their eyes on the ground before them, the risk for falling is far greater.

To sustain momentum, you have to teach your team to focus on the nearest goal. For a football team, that is the next game. If you're just gaining momentum, the nearest goal may be establishing each team member's role or, if you already have a good head of steam, focusing the team's energies on completing a current project with excellence or serving a current client with the utmost respect and professionalism.

There's nothing new about taking one step at a time—however, the difference for a championship coach is that one misstep can adversely affect the team's ability to reach the big goal. If a highly ranked college football team loses one game, the players must rely on the failure of their competition to meet their overall goal. You've probably heard coaches lament, "Well, all we can do now is win every game from here on out and hope for some help." That's an unenviable place to be.

To keep your team's fate in its own hands, the players have to solely focus on meeting the nearest goal so that when they reach the final push, they will still be rolling with confidence. The best way to accomplish this is to make sure you spend more time promoting the goal at hand. There's nothing wrong with reminding the team that the championship is waiting in the wings, but the leader has to be careful; too much talk of the overall goal, and the smaller goals become lost in the light.

To help your team appreciate one victory at a time, promote one step at a time. Short of the days before the championship, the only time the leader should be talking up the overall goal is the initial moment following a successful step. This serves as a celebratory reminder that the team has moved one step closer to home. But soon after, the leader must redeploy the team's energies on the task at hand.

Lesson 3: Teach Them to Treat Every Challenge the Same.

Underestimating the challenge before your team is likely the biggest momentum killer. Every year, the eight coaches enter the season with high, nationwide expectations from the media and hordes of fans. They are expected to win all of their games, especially the "easy" ones. Although expectations can be a confidence builder, they can also promote a false security.

Favored teams have the odds on their side, but they also face a greater temptation to cruise. When a team tries to conserve fuel, it becomes more susceptible to failure. That's because momentum doesn't sustain itself. It must be continually fueled.

Every team experiences friction on the path to the big goal. Sometimes the friction is high—maybe the next game is against the defending champion—and the team knows its engine must be firing at full speed to secure victory. Other times the friction is low—maybe the next opponent is the last-place team—and although a full head of steam isn't necessary to win, the teammates become easier to defeat if they slow their pace too much. A championship coach ensures that a great team does not underestimate a small challenge.

Keeping your team's engine running full steam is a matter of not differentiating the challenges. It's a matter of teaching the members to see every challenge as a great challenge and overcoming it as a great victory. Coach McCartney maintained, "You have to get [your team] to think: *If there is just somehow, some way we can win this game by one point, it would be the greatest victory that I've ever been a part of.*"

To help a team treat every challenge the same, it would be easiest (but not honest) for a leader to exaggerate the extent of each challenge. However, for most leaders this isn't an option on more than just the integrity account. The eight championship coaches, for instance, have teams with full access to the media and ESPN, giving their players a full understanding of whether their current challenge is a formidable one. In most cases, the coach does not have to stress the difficulty of a task; the real challenge lies in getting the team up for an easy opponent. The best coaches do this by stressing the importance of maintaining a high level of play throughout the season, regardless of the challenge.

> "My job was to get my team on one heartbeat."
> —GENE STALLINGS

Coach Stallings was explicit in describing how he went about this. "First of all, you gotta win the games you're supposed to win," he said.

> If you don't think playing Chattanooga is an important game, just lose to Chattanooga. Then you'll see how important Chattanooga is.
>
> I never put more emphasis on one team than I did another . . . I personally never worried about the opponent. I didn't care where we played, who we played, or what time we played; I care less about those things. My job was to get my team on one heartbeat. My job was to get my team ready to play. I never did try to think that my scheme was better than your scheme. I just thought my player would play better than your player.

His method is one that every leader should emulate. To treat every challenge the same, Stallings didn't talk up who they were playing or where they were traveling or what time of day they were playing. In essence, he didn't talk up the challenge; he talked up his team. By not stressing the details of the challenge and instead focusing his teams on the tasks they needed to accomplish to win, he empowered them with two essentials for team victory: unity and confidence. With these in their arsenal, teams are equipped to sustain momentum week in and week out.

Lesson 4: Teach Them to Perform with Relaxed Confidence.

"Success breeds success," Coach Osborne said. Confidence has a positive effect on momentum. As a team continues to succeed, the members become increasingly trusting of the system of preparation and execution that the leader has established. Then they are more likely to relax and perform with poise.

The Huskers "prepared the same each week," explained Coach Osborne. "Even if we were a fifty-point favorite, it didn't make any difference; we still prepared the same. And as a result we seldom got upset by somebody we should have beaten."

Osborne's explanation indicates that a team's confidence is not grounded in mere hype; it springs from consistent actions that consistently produce success. It is the leader's job to define these actions and then prepare his team to carry them out with excellence each week. We're not talking about creating ruts here; we're talking about sustaining streaks. We're talking about the reinforcing effects of strategic repetition.

I spoke with Coach Coker midseason about this, and he was very confident in his answer:

> We will win the game on Tuesday that everybody wants us to win on Saturday when we come out through the smoke . . . There are

no major pep talks, no magic words that you can say then. Maybe that will work one time and possibly twice, but you have ten more games to play, so what are you going to do then? The big thing is knowing that we are extremely prepared. Knowing that gives us confidence for Saturday.

When a team sees that doing something a certain way produces success—once, twice, then three times and beyond—it is the leader's job to encapsulate that action and empower his team to repeat it every week, from how it prepares for a challenge to how it executes its tasks in the midst of the challenge. The result: sustaining momentum becomes a natural occurrence as the team becomes more familiar with the steps to success. This may be the reason momentum seems so whimsical; out of nowhere, a team just seems to possess it. The truth, however, is that the actions that make a team successful the first time merely become more instinctive. When I was a coach, I used to call this playing with relaxed confidence.

> Sustaining momentum becomes a natural occurrence as the team becomes more familiar with the steps to success. This may be the reason momentum seems so whimsical.

Sustaining Momentum Means Playing with Confidence

If you watch any sports on TV, you've probably heard the announcer praise a player's "poise" on the field. He's referring to the player's ability to continually perform at a high level despite the pressure and distractions of a game. A team with relaxed confidence accomplishes the same thing week in and week out.

One way the great Coach Wooden did this was by teaching his players, "Be quick, but don't hurry."[5] Here is what that means.

To "be quick," a team must be totally prepared. To this end, Coach Wooden was meticulous with every detail, down to how his teams should wear their socks to guard against blisters and tie their shoes so they would never come unlaced during a game. With detailed preparation, he kept his teams unencumbered in the midst of their endeavors. Free to perform efficiently, they were then able to anticipate situations before they arose. Doing this allowed them to react confidently and kept them from making hurried miscalculations. Once this became habit, Wooden's teams sustained unmatched momentum for a decade.

Every great coach knows that when teams are both confident and relaxed, they will perform at the highest level. This is precisely how Coach Fulmer's '98 Volunteers won their national championship. He reminisced with me:

> We sustained momentum very well that particular year because we never worried about the next opponent. We just got ready for this Monday's practice, this Tuesday's practice. We didn't worry about Wednesday's practice or Thursday's. We worried about today . . . We didn't look at the championship game either, although everybody wanted you to and it was what they wanted to talk about—particularly when we had the seven, eight, or nine wins. But in the midst of that we still stayed the course as a team.

If you observe the most prolific coaches, you'll find the one thing they have in common is an ability to instill confidence in their teams. That, above all, seemed to be the one mutual result all eight coaches achieved while sustaining their championship runs.

The lesson thus far is that preparation that instills confidence seems to be the best combination for maintaining momentum, despite the many distractions that arise over the course of an endeavor.

Yet in truth, we cannot talk about sustaining momentum for the long haul without discussing a leader's ability to cultivate his team's confidence through the good times *and* the bad. In short, it is not just their confident, consistent actions that keep a team moving forward full steam; it is also their confident, consistent *reactions* to success and failure—their morale. This issue requires its own chapter.

4

Morale

Then someone walked up next to me, and I could only stare at his feet. It was the senior, All-American fullback. He leaned over on his knees, looked me in the eye, and said, "Rookie, run with me."

—Coach Mullins

I think it's important for the coach to spread the praise to all the players . . . I'm not good at trying to build up a guy just for the honor or the All-Americans.

—Coach Spurrier, University of Florida
1996 National Champions

It is always a challenge," admitted Coach Fulmer, "perhaps the ultimate challenge for any coach." We were discussing team morale and a coach's responsibility to maintain it. He is correct to categorize it that way. I remember failing miserably at the challenge with my most successful high school team.

We were undefeated and ranked number one in the state at the end of the regular season. We were a shoo-in to win state. There was only one problem. Our state playoffs were structured with a northern and a southern division in Palm Beach County. We were from the northern division, and there was another team from the southern division that was also undefeated in conference play. The rule was that if you had two undefeated teams in conference play that had not played each other that particular year, you would alternate who went to the state playoffs. Since a team from the northern division had represented Palm Beach County the previous year, the team from the southern division got to go instead of us, even though we were ranked number one in the state.

I'd be lying if I told you it wasn't a letdown. The guys on the team were upset and felt it was entirely unfair. I agreed, but I still hoped to reward them for a fine season. A few days later I was approached by a bowl committee from northern Florida that was arranging some high school bowl games. Since we would not be going to state, the committee asked if we would like to play in a bowl game?

When I asked some team leaders about it, they had mixed feelings. "Why should we play?" they lamented. "Weren't the other teams below us?" Some of the guys wanted to play anyway, and others were mad that it was their only option. It was a tough decision, but I thought about it and figured the game was a good way to reward the guys. I contacted the bowl committee and accepted. I knew my team felt slighted, but I thought at least the guys could go pound on a team in a bowl game and end the season on a more positive note.

We found out the team we would play had missed the state playoffs by one game. We knew it was a decent team, but when my staff watched the first game film, we realized that it wasn't nearly as good as ours; in fact, playing that team would be a cakewalk. We didn't mess with watching any more film, and we didn't implement new strategy for the game. We went about our normal business, knowing our team was superior and would have no problem winning.

We were wrong. We stepped onto that field and got ourselves beat. The players' hearts and minds were not in the game, and it was my fault. I overlooked the importance of team morale.

Afterward I found out that not only were some of the guys unhappy about playing in the bowl game in the first place, but everyone was still very disappointed that the team wasn't allowed to defend its number one ranking at state. They felt that the game was a shoddy concession, and looking back, we probably never should have played. At the very least, I should have addressed the issues long before letting the team take the field again. As a result of my shortsightedness and the team's dampened morale, we ended the finest season in the high school's history with a disheartening loss. The memory of the perfect season was forever tainted.

That year I learned that maintaining morale is a critical responsibility for any leader because without it, a team quickly loses its footing, no matter how stable it seems. This cuts momentum short, and it makes performing at an optimal level almost impossible. Ignored completely, low morale can implode a team. My example is a case in point. Our coaching staff felt our team had something to prove by playing that bowl game, but the notion proved far less substantial than the players' disappointment. As a result, we ended a special season on a sour note.

To instill and maintain high morale, a coach must nurture his team's confidence in good times and bad. Above all, he must keep the team positive.

In success, a leader cannot take a team's morale for granted. This is the mistake I made with my team. In essence, I assumed the players were fine since we had such a great season. The truth was a different story.

In failure, the team has to know it's not the end. A great coach acknowledges that mistakes are disappointing, but conveys that success can come around the next bend. He knows how to give the team hope when circumstances seem bleak or disheartening. When I was a freshman in high school, I had a coach who did this well, even at the height of frustration.

I made the varsity team as the starting strong safety, but I was also asked to be the backup punter. We were playing down in Cincinnati when our punter was injured, and I was called on for the first time. I was psyched up; I told myself I was gonna kill the ball and set a record on my first kick. The ball was snapped, and I caught it cleanly. I released the ball in what I thought was perfect position and swung my leg through with everything I had.

Have you ever seen that *Peanuts* cartoon where Lucy keeps yanking the football from the path of Charlie Brown's foot just before he can kick a field goal? That was me, minus Lucy. As my leg swung through the space where the ball should have been, I looked up, and my foot missed the ball. I didn't shank it to one side. I missed the ball completely, and like good ole Chuck, I fell flat on my back.

The ball trickled forward between a linesman's legs, and the other team jumped on it. I will never forget looking to the bench and seeing my coach calling me everything he could think of. He slammed his hat down and started stomping on it with all 250 pounds. My only salvation was that the defense stayed on the field so I didn't have to face his wrath at close range. He was ripping mad for sure; but despite his obvious—and warranted—frustration, his wisdom shone through. He didn't let his emotions undermine the importance of nurturing my confidence. The next time our team was forced to punt, without a word about my debacle, he put me right back in. And that time I didn't let him down.

The foundation of maintaining morale is hope. It's passing on the perspective that a team or an individual on the team can always succeed with the next step—the next game, the next practice, the next pass. In general, the coach offers this through his confidence in his players, the way my high school coach offered it to me. But practically speaking, there's more to it. A leader can take proactive steps to maintain his team's confidence and give hope in any circumstance.

Boosting and Bolstering Team Spirit

To determine the necessary steps to maintaining high morale, I sought the advice of the eight national champions whose circumstances are arguably as difficult as any leader's. Not only are they forced to deal with the prospect of success and failure on a weekly basis, but their highly publicized teams are stacked with high school All-Americans and MVPs. This situation can quickly turn their locker rooms into breeding grounds for morale problems if they are not proactive about the issue.

Though I talked with the coaches separately, I found that their recommendations fashion five common actions that every leader should take to build up and reinforce team confidence. Keep in mind that these are *proactive* steps that should ideally be implemented *before* morale problems exist. If your team is already struggling, these steps will remedy the problem, but the team may need a little longer to come around.

Action 1: Reiterate Team Goals Before Every Endeavor.

The paradox of team morale is that it represents the outlook of a *group,* but it is established by *individual* viewpoints. The key, then, is to sway individual viewpoints to a mutual position. In particular, when teammates share a common outlook on the following things, morale tends to remain high:

- *Vision.* When teammates begin using the phrase "our team," the bond is deepening. This language indicates that individuals see the team as a unit and reaching the team goals as a unified endeavor, not an individualistic enterprise.

- *Responsibility.* When teammates accept that each has a role to play in success, true accountability can take place between them. This increases their vulnerability with one another and takes their bond to a more intimate level.

- *Sacrifice.* Mutual sacrifice is the quickest way to deepen a team's bond. When teammates see one member give his all for the team, others are inspired to do the same. Soon, teammates don't see their own accomplishments outside the value they add to the team's effort.

As a freshman trying to make Georgetown's team, I experienced the effects of a common outlook on these principles, and it made a lasting impression. During tryouts, they fed us to the lions every day. We were regularly pitted against guys—men, really—who just returned from Vietnam. These upperclassmen were tough and strong and intimidating. To make matters worse, the philosophy of our coaches, as I told you earlier, was to let fights separate the boys from the men, and fights broke out frequently during drills. They often allowed the upperclassmen to beat on the freshmen, to harass us and see if they could break our spirits. This method seems archaic now, but it was effective. The number of freshmen dropped by the hour.

One practice when the fights were particularly heavy, I was standing with a few other freshmen including this kid named Berkich, from eastern Kentucky, with a heavy accent. On the heels of another fight, he leaned over to us and said, "Break down, boys, and huddle up; thair gunna keel us all." We had a good laugh, but at the same time we sensed the significance of his words. Specifically they pointed out the one thing that we freshmen had in common: we were trying to survive. Despite our different viewpoints, we had a common outlook. For that group of us eighteen- and nineteen-year-olds, every practice was more than a tryout; it was a survival test.

After that day, a noticeable thing happened. The group of freshmen became very close. We began to encourage each other, to share responsibility, to pick each other up when we got knocked down, to make sacrifices for each other. Most freshmen during that brutal summer didn't make it more than a week—only about fifteen of sixty-five made the team. But as it so happened, it was that group of us who bonded over a common outlook and managed to survive together. Because our individual viewpoints found common ground, we all reached our goal.

Common outlooks like that build unity, and unity raises morale. As leaders, we have the job to regularly remind the team of its common outlook, like Berkich did for us freshmen. When we do, teammates will tend to close the gaps between them.

Action 2: Maintain Uniform Leadership.

When I spoke with Coach Fulmer about team morale, he concluded,

> I think it goes back to the consistency of your assistant coaches. I have to be consistent in how I present myself first . . . but the presentations that are given [to the team] from the support groups on a daily basis have to be consistent.
>
> We've been pretty fortunate to keep most of our coaches here. I've also put a lot of stock into the leadership of the seniors and the upperclassmen, and so far we've been fortunate to have some really good, solid kids. From that standpoint, they have truly been an extension of the coaching staff to the team and from the team to the coaching staff.

When the leaders of a team are on the same page, maintaining high morale is a much easier assignment. There is minimal contradiction in how team members are treated and continuity in how the team responds to the spectrum of victory and defeat. This allows teammates to conform their attitudes and actions to the same standard.

The basic advantage of consistent leadership is conveying a consistent message—one that helps rule out false expectations and solidify a unified front. United hearts and minds lead to united motives and actions. Coach Osborne achieved this masterfully by attaching a specific theme to each game that the players could rally around.

"We used something that we picked up from the Kansas City Chiefs called a theme of the week," he explained.

> Maybe it would be courage or handling adversity or compassion. Every week I would usually get various people, maybe athletic, political, or religious figures, to flesh out the theme. We would then discuss [for example] what courage was and how to have physical and relational courage. Then we would talk about that specific theme during the week, and it would be represented in the scouting report. In a season of fourteen or fifteen different weeks, we would have fourteen or fifteen different themes, each having to do with different character issues. This essentially led to an understanding that when the team won, everybody won, and when the team lost, everybody lost.

In his innovative fashion, Coach Osborne used character building as a tactic to maintain team morale over the entire season. Each week's theme was consistently communicated by the leadership and therefore became the center of the team's motivation and activity. This tactic tightened the team's bond, and it fortified the team's performance as teammates kindled their efforts with the same fuel. It's pioneering advice for any leader to model.

Action 3: Define Each Team Member's Role in Success.

"I spoke with authority," explained Coach Stallings. "The player knew his limitations and boundaries, where he could go and where he couldn't go. We had a job to do. I was always fair with a player and made sure he understood that. But at the same time, I always worked within the framework of the rules for every player. [As a result] I just never had any problems with team unity. I can't ever remember having a good player that didn't play his best."

Coach Stallings's teams never struggled with low morale because his players always understood what was expected of them; and what was expected was nothing more than they could contribute. Like any great leader, Stallings helped his players comprehend the scope of their abilities and then clarified their function in the grander scheme. Doing this perpetuated the following emotions:

- A sense of ownership in the team's success
- A sense of responsibility to do their part

These emotions, felt team-wide, epitomize the product of high morale.

While an assistant coach at the University of Michigan, Coach McCartney witnessed how his predecessor advanced the same sentiments:

I had the good fortune to work under Bo Schembechler for eight and a half years. The thing that he would do that was just so masterful is that every kid that came down to Michigan, he went into their home and they came into his home. He brought every kid in three times a year to interview them and to dialogue with them on what was really going on in their life. He would then tell them his impressions—he'd be very forthright and very candid in his impressions of their performance. He was always challenging them.

. . . To me, coaching is taking a guy where he can't take himself; and if you're going to lead someone today with all of the complex problems that exist out there, you have got to know his world. And he's got to know that he's welcome in your house. This is what I saw Bo Schembechler do. As a result, when we had team meetings, he could call guys out. He would just single them out and say, "This is what I need to you do."

As successful coaches, Schembechler and McCartney understood something that many leaders don't; they understood that there *is* something personal about team success, but it's not personal recognition. It's personal responsibility.

When each player hears his coach tell him the team needs him for a specific purpose, he is compelled to excel not for personal glory but for a sense of duty to his teammates. This should be regarded not as manipulation but as accountability. High morale is based on a "we-need-you/you-need-us" mind-set. And to spread it team-wide, these regular practices are required:

- Honest evaluation of talent

- Specific explanation of purpose

- Sharp observation of progress

Each ingredient calls for gut-level candor with team members not only on the front end before an endeavor begins but also during the course of each undertaking. "Perhaps," explained Coach McCartney, "you have a kid that you say, 'Look, son, you are a good passer, but we're going to win this game not necessarily by using that skill; and you're going to have to hand the ball off more; and your receivers are going to have to block more this week because these guys are going to double cover us the whole game. If our running game is effective, they won't be able to stop us.'"

Team confidence can grow when team members comprehend and accept their roles in each challenge. Helping them understand that their roles might change for the good of the team allows them to internalize responsibility in a personal-but-not-conceited way.

> There is something personal about team success, but it's not personal recognition. It's personal responsibility

And that, as Coach Stallings explained, is a must:

> Let's say that our goal is to be a good third-down team. Well, that doesn't mean diddlysquat unless you find out that the reason you weren't a good third-down team from the beginning was because the wide receivers ran the wrong route or the quarterback overthrew the receiver or the offensive line didn't protect the quarterback. Now in order to make that third down better, the right guard is going to have to protect the quarterback. That means something to someone. Or you might tell the receiver that he has to run a proper route. That means something to someone. [Team unity] has got to come down to the individual player, or it doesn't mean anything. If winning is going to mean anything, the players have got to understand that they were a part of it.

Action 4: Promote Mutual Respect.

Speaking of character building, the thematic umbrella of team morale is respect—an effective team is fully sheltered by it. "It's about what we can do together," explained Coach McCartney. "You could have a great game, you could have a maximum performance, and you could break all of your own personal records, but if we don't win the game, all those things are empty, they're shallow . . . [Consider] the tiger versus the lion. One on one, the tiger will win every time. The tiger family is very selfish. But if there are ten lions and ten tigers, the lions will win every time because the lions care about each other, and really that's what it takes."

The coach who can teach his players to think of their teammates first sets them up to share in both success and failure. For instance, what would be the difference if a kicker who missed a field goal heard his teammates build him back up, tell him it was okay—he'd get another shot? Wouldn't he be less burdened about his mistake?

Wouldn't he be more confident to succeed with his next opportunity? Of course he would.

"What I've learned in coaching," confessed McCartney, "is 'I got your back; I got you covered.'" This idea is the essence of mutual respect, and it begins with the knowledge that no single person can make or break the team. This does not exclude the leader, as Coach Stoops points out to his Sooners:

> We emphasize quite often that the team is always more important than the individual, and that if you remove any one of us, the team is still going to go on and succeed and do awfully well. That starts with me. You take me out of here, and we're still going to do well. Oklahoma football is much more than one individual, and we talk about that. We talk about caring and humility.
>
> You know, we have been fortunate. Some of our best players in the last several years, [especially] when we won the national championship, have [understood] this. Josh Heupel, who was the AP Player of the Year and was an All-American and runner-up for the Heisman, is a truly humble team person. So when you have your best players like Quentin Griffin, Rocky Calmus, Roy Williams—you know, Butkus Award winners, Jim Thorpe Award winners—when you have these great players that are genuinely this way, they set a great example that lasts for quite a while with your teams. They understand that the team is what really matters and that winning championships is what you remember most, not individual accomplishments.

Stoops' comment substantiates the point. Mutual respect makes a team a team. And it spreads best from the top down.

"I have to be consistent first in how I present myself—in the example I set," concurred Coach Fulmer. Then from the assistant coaches to the team leaders to the role players to the practice squad, the seed of respect spreads like a vine and knits the team together. When the coach confesses his need of each player and the players confess their need of each other, team morale is rooted and steadfast.

I'll never forget the star running back at Georgetown College. He exemplified the leadership we're talking about, and it had a huge impact on me.

During the initial practices, the coaches worked us like dogs, and nearing the end of the second day, I was unsure of myself. I was on my last leg, literally, and then they lined us up to run 40-yard wind sprints. I bent over with my hands on my knees and took deep breaths, trying to keep my lunch down. I wondered for the first time if I could make it. Then someone walked up next to me, and I could only stare at his feet. It was the senior, All-American fullback. He leaned over on his knees, looked me in the eye, and said, "Rookie, run with me."

I was spent—but I stood up straight, and when the whistle blew again, I stayed right next to him. When he ran faster, I ran faster. I didn't stop until he stopped. Somehow I survived those sprints; but something much more important took place. Because of Charley's respect for me, I became more than an underclassman that day; I became a teammate. It made all the difference in the world.

Action 5: Spread Your Praise Around.

"In order for somebody to have ownership of something," Coach McCartney asserted, "you have to acknowledge their contribution." This goes for the whole team.

Coach Spurrier had a unique method of going about this. "I publicly praise players that do not get much attention like guards and down linemen," he admitted. "Players that everyone knows as the star players are the quarterbacks, receivers, linebackers, whoever kicks, and so forth. But I think it's important for the coach to spread the praise to all the players . . . I'm not good at trying to build up a guy just for the honor or the All-Americans."

His advice is innovative for raising the spirit of a team, because unappreciated team members rarely retain a group mentality. To counterbalance their feelings of inadequacy, they strive for personal recognition instead of team success, often regardless of how that affects the team's outcome. Having a team with this attitude then makes it nearly impossible to attack an endeavor with single-minded focus.

His advice doesn't mean leaders should avoid utilizing their best players more often than others. It also doesn't mean leaders should avoid giving time to their best players. What we're talking about here is the allocation of a leader's praise, and it should always be spread widely to the team so that everyone senses he plays a role in success.

In fact, Coach Spurrier's insight might argue that it is often wise to spread more praise to the lesser-known teammates because the best players need less affirmation.

Remember Skinny Carl? His story illustrates this principle precisely. When I took the time to build him up and gave him opportunities to succeed in front of his teammates, their spirits were lifted along with his. They saw the tremendous value he gave to the team, and they rallied their efforts around his.

It's a fact that a leader does not have to tell his team who the stars are. All members can see for themselves. Therefore, he does not have to channel his praise to the upper echelon. He can let actions speak for themselves and share his praise with the behind-the-scenes majority who work hard and unnoticed for the good of the team. It shows all team members that their actions influence the team's success, and it shows the stars that they can't be their best by themselves. This is an important final step.

There are certainly other methods a leader can use to maintain high team morale, but all go through a process by which teammates come to see the same path to success, accept responsibility for their roles, and learn to value each other. These are the keys to keeping a team's spirits high and each member's mind focused on what's most important. But if we're honest, a team needs something more to continually succeed.

Many upbeat, self-sacrificing teams end up failing more than they should because they don't possess a specific, hands-on strategy for each endeavor. Think of it this way: a team with high morale is a team with the loftiest intentions and the best attitudes—all integral to success. Yet without a specific plan for winning, good intentions and great attitudes will carry a team only so far.

I'll show you what I mean.

5

Game Planning

We meet with our staff two weeks before practice every August. We go out to what we call the hideaway, a cottage or somewhere where nobody can get in touch with us—no phones or anything. We take all our staff and go over every detail of what we're going to do that year.

—COACH BOWDEN, Florida State University
1993 and 1999 National Champions

The opposing coach got so frustrated, he called a time-out and charged the referee to indict us. He claimed we tapped into his headset and were listening to him and his coaches discuss plays. "You guys are cheating!" he yelled.

—COACH MULLINS

A mentally prepared team has a "step up" on the competition. But a team still has to physically perform. On this second truth, many teams fall short of greatness. Teammates are motivated and unified to win; they possess the talent to succeed; but then they fail to execute an effective plan. One of the most common reasons for this unfortunate outcome is that a coach is easily tempted to rely on talent alone to carry the team to victory. Championship coaches know this temptation well. In their national championship runs, each of the eight coaches possessed a trio of superstars on his team. See if any of these names ring a bell:

| Coach Coker's 2001 Team | Ken Dorsey, Clinton Portis, Jeremy Shockey |

Coach Stoops's 2000 Team	Josh Heupel, Rocky Calmus, Quentin Griffin
Coach Bowden's 1999 Team	Peter Warrick, Sebastian Janikowski, Chris Weinke
Coach Fulmer's 1998 Team	Al Wilson, Peerless Price, Jamal Lewis
Coach Osborne's 1997 Team	Ahman Green, Grant Wistrom, Jason Peter
Coach Spurrier's 1996 Team	Danny Wuerffel, Fred Taylor, Jevon Kearse
Coach Osborne's 1995 Team	Tommie Frazier, Ahman Green, Grant Wistrom
Coach Osborne's 1994 Team	Lawrence Philips, Tommie Frazier, Brook Berringer
Coach Bowden's 1993 Team	Charlie Ward, Derrick Brooks, Warrick Dunn
Coach Stallings's 1992 Team	George Teague, John Copeland, Eric Curry
Coach McCartney's 1990 Team	Eric Bieniemy, Alfred Williams, Joe Garten

With players like these, it's tempting to lean on their talent. But the eight coaches understand that more talent doesn't guarantee more success. In fact, upsets occur when the underdog outwits the more talented team that fails to prepare. Remember my undefeated high school team that lost its final bowl game? Not only did I fail to address the team's shriveled morale, but I thought our superior talent was enough to carry our team to success. I was wrong on two accounts.

A Team Needs a Plan

The truth is that success always takes more planning than performing, especially when it involves a team. Coach Bear Bryant once confessed that the typical fan has little concept of the amount of time that goes into planning a single football game. "I tell my players," he said, "our staff will study, prepare, and plan one hour for every minute the players are on the football field."

If you're doing the math, that means sixty hours went into planning one game. I wonder how many leaders give half as much time to planning a single endeavor.

In Chapter 4, I mentioned Coach Bryant's influence on Coach Bowden's preparation-centered leadership and how that has helped his Seminoles sustain unmatched consistency over the last three decades. What I didn't mention is the extent to which Bowden goes to plan for games.

He explained this further:

> We meet with our staff two weeks before practice every August. We go out to what we call the hideaway, a cottage or somewhere where nobody can get in touch with us—no phones or anything. We take all our staff and go over every detail of what we're going to do that year. We decide on the snap count and how we're going to line up. We discuss how we plan to handle every situation we might face . . . We discuss our training rules. Then I'll bring in doctors, businessmen, drug experts, and law enforcement people to talk to our staff.

As he indicates, game planning for Coach Bowden begins by preparing for every conceivable situation the team might face, on and off the field. His is an important point because it illustrates that game planning must be more specific than simply recasting a vision. It takes more time and much thought—two things many leaders sacrifice in the name of productivity. In fact, the tendency with today's hustle-faced, do-it-now approach to tasks is to get the planning out of the way so the doing can begin. But haste is the downside of ambition.

So many people labor under the whip of quotas and deadlines that taking more time to plan seems only to compound the problem by leaving less time to act. *All those details? Who has time? We'll just Indiana Jones our way through it, making it up as we go along.* This too common mind-set among today's leaders leaves teams wide open for chaos and confusion.

The collegiate coach knows this well because he does not have the potential grace of extensions when he realizes his team is not prepared. For a coach, the time line for success is inflexible. In most cases, he has one week to get his team ready and sixty minutes to lead it to victory. Game day means game on; and if the players are not prepared, they're in for a long day and a lot of disappointment. Coaches may learn quickly the necessity of effective game planning. At the least, there's no doubt they are excellent sources of insight on the topic.

The Benefits

In general, the eight coaches pointed out several benefits that thorough game planning provides teams *before* they tackle an endeavor. We've touched on a few of these in the previous chapters, but they bear repeating briefly here under this new light before we talk about how to create a game plan.

Effective game planning provides . . .

Confidence. Where a team's pace is concerned, players will be only as efficient as the least efficient player. If one teammate is uncertain about his role, the team's tempo will be slowed. On the other hand, when players know precisely what is expected of them as a function of the game plan, the team can act in unison without hesitation. A plan gives confidence.

Direction. On the football field, speed hurts a team if a player is running the wrong way, strength slows a team if a player is not using it properly, and size gets in the way if a player is just standing around.

A team's players need clear direction in order to maximize their talents. Otherwise, they'll just get in each other's way. A game plan shows the team not only how it will succeed but also how each player's talents will be employed in success.

Focus. Without a game plan, a team's eyes tend to wander. Teammates look for what *will come* if they are successful instead of what *needs to be done* to be successful. With a game plan, a team's eyes turn to the one goal before it. For a football team, this means one game; for your team, it may mean one project or one organization or one person. The point is that a game plan keeps the team's attention on what needs to be done now.

Unity. Working together doesn't happen by an act of will; it happens when teammates combine their many talents to reach one goal. In other words, unity is not a decision; it is an action. A game plan shows a team how to pool resources and proceed in unified fashion.

Accountability. A coach cannot see how every player is performing, nor can he enter the huddle before every play and correct what players did wrong. In his place, the game plan serves as the team's omnipotent standard of all activity. Actions within the game plan are acceptable; actions outside the game plan are not. When teammates understand this, they can help each other observe the standard in the heat of battle.

In sum, when an effective game plan is communicated to the team, it conveys why the teammates should do it, how they are going to do it, and what they can expect in the process of doing it. To answer these questions is an essential task of a leader.

The Creation of a Game Plan

Most people can see *how* an effective game plan can help a team. Creating one is a different story.

Because collegiate coaches typically craft more game plans in a half-year period than most leaders, I sought out the advice of the eight national champions hoping to glean some greater insight. I asked the coaches how they go (or went) about the process of planning for their games. Their answers provide us with four steps for creating effective game plans for our teams.

Step 1: Distinguish Your Biggest Obstacles.

"First," explained Coach Fulmer, "we define who the teams are that we have to beat year in and year out, and the non-conference teams that are really good—like this year we played Miami. You try to focus on the recruiting, the off season, the planning, and philosophical changes needed to be made in order to win those ball games."

At the championship level, winning every game is vital—and each coach reiterated the fact—but they also admitted that their games against formidable opponents always loom the largest. Since they have the greatest potential to derail a championship-bound team, the leader must determine what they are and then prepare his team accordingly to meet the challenge. This may require, as Coach Fulmer alluded, adjusting anything from recruiting to leadership philosophy. For each team, the appropriate response is decidedly different, but what remains consistent is the need for extra attention to the team's biggest obstacles.

When I asked Coach Bowden about how he prepares for his biggest rivals each year, he admitted that it was necessary to treat those games differently without downplaying the other games:

Well, the best thing to do is to take one game at a time. However, yes, if we're playing Florida and we have a team in front of them that's not up to the same caliber, we might sneak in a few things that week, but we won't tell our kids. If they ever get the idea that

68

you don't think this team you're playing is serious, they're going to get upset. But we might sneak in a couple plays that week before Florida or Miami to work on them. We don't tell the kids, "Hey, boys, this is what we use for Miami!" . . . but we [the coaches] might peek ahead some. Another thing [we do] is that usually when we play Florida and Miami, we'll break down every film. For example, if they've played ten games before us, we'll look at ten films. For everybody else, we only look at three or four.

It's for good reason that Coach Bowden's game-planning efforts intensify when he plays Florida and Miami. If you look at the history of FSU's games versus either rival, many national championships were affected by the outcomes. In fact, Miami's run to repeat in 2002 was nearly ruined by a struggling but well-prepared Florida State team. If you remember, Coach Bowden's team had the number-one-ranked 'Canes on the ropes for most of the game, and had it not been for a missed last-second field goal, FSU would have pulled off the upset. Despite his team's survival, the Seminoles' effort made a lasting impression on Coach Coker. "That was probably the greatest football game I have ever been around," he told me. "The most phenomenal game I have ever been around in my life. The thing that was so phenomenal was that they never flinched; they never, never did."

Because Coach Bowden distinguishes his team's biggest obstacles each year, he is able to adjust his game-planning efforts so that even an ominous obstacle like the defending-champion Hurricanes is a viable win for his team.

Coach McCartney employed a similar strategy:

In the summer you had to identify key games where, if you didn't do something special and prepare in advance, there would never be enough time in one week. For example, let's say that we are playing Nebraska in week seven. I know that only one week is not enough time to [prepare], so what I would do is this: during two-day practices, which last two weeks, I would begin to implement some of the things that I had to really reinforce that week [we played Nebraska] without telling the players that I was working on Nebraska. One week is not enough time to do it, so you plan ahead. You're going to need maximum performance, and you have to be able to give yourself a chance to get that.

The common insight offered by Coaches Fulmer, Bowden, and McCartney seems to fly in the face of previous advice offered in this book—namely, the concept of focusing on one game at a time—and in a way, it does. But as each indicated, this is something leaders must do, if at all possible, without full explanation to their teams in order to maintain their focus. It's not a matter of deception; it's a matter of protection. It's like the father who asks his young child to trust him when he tells the boy it is best that he not wander from his side. The father would rather not prematurely explain to the young boy the dangers of the world, lest he focus on the dangers and lose his childhood to fear. He would rather teach the boy not to wander off and, in so doing, keep him out of danger until he is ready to face it on his own.

The leader must walk a fine line to prepare his team ahead of time and still keep his players focused on what's before them, but it's a step that must be taken because some challenges require more than standard practice.

Step 2: Define Your Strengths.

"Once you decide on your approach for the offense, defense, and special teams," said Coach Fulmer, "it's a matter of . . . working on your personnel and trying to maximize your strengths. In every way you can, you find those little differences that end up being the difference in winning ball games. So much of it goes back to the off season when we worked on strength and conditioning."

In my fifteen years of coaching, I observed many coaches who didn't change their game strategies and systems when their talent changed. As a result, their teams weakened over time, and they found themselves very frustrated. From these observations, I gathered that a good coach should probably never be locked into any one game plan until he determined his strengths in each situation. If I had a quarterback with a strong arm, for instance, who couldn't run very well, I designed an offense that gave him protection when he dropped back and required little movement so he didn't have to worry about using his feet. If I had a quarterback like Michael Vick with quick feet, then I created a system that gave him a lot more flexibility to take advantage of his running ability.

The leadership principle is this: understand your team's strengths in each endeavor, and then design your game plan around those strengths. Often we spend more time trying to strengthen our weaknesses in the name of becoming more balanced. This approach takes much longer and is less effective because it takes the focus off our strengths. And victory always comes by exploiting our strengths, not by improving our weaknesses.

Step 3: Determine Their Weaknesses.

"Every summer," Coach Bowden explained,

I make my coaching staff turn a scouting report in to me on all the teams that we play . . . so I can read those reports and get a little bit of an idea what we're facing that year. Then we study the film and try to find out the best way to attack the other teams and how to defend against them. We figure out anything we need to know to help us win the ball game. Then we try to tweak a little bit here and a little bit there so that we will take advantage of that other team's weaknesses. In other words, as we study their films, we're looking for a flaw; we're looking for a mistake. They might have a tackle that should be playing with his inside arm but has a steady spell with his outside arm. And he leaves a vacancy there so you try to take advantage of that. They might have a slow corner and a fast corner so we might throw all day long on that slow corner and not even test the other guy. Those are the things we're looking for.

Remember my earlier story about beating Fort Pierce Central and the team chanting, "We won because we worked harder! We won because we worked harder!" Well, one of the ways we worked harder was by studying film to uncover chinks in the other team's armor. One weakness that we discovered in Fort Pierce was their long snapper. He had poor technique and a weak arm, and his ball to the punter was slow and wobbly, so we decided to capitalize on it. We decided that every time the other team punted, we were going for the block.

That week we rehearsed a variety of punt-block formations until we were confident of each one. Our plan paid off big-time. During that game, we blocked two Fort Pierce punts and scored a touchdown on one of them. Those blocked punts played a big part in our 39-6 victory over a team with superior talent.

The fact is that the competition always has weaknesses—even the toughest competition. No team is without flaws. Though they may be small or obscure, it's your job as the leader to expose them and introduce them into your team's game plan.

Step 4: Have a Backup Plan Ready.

"We generally have an overall plan that we think suits our personnel and what's best for us," explained Coach Spurrier. "Then a lot of times . . . we get into the game, and it may change. Because of that, I think our plan was more flexible than a lot of other teams.

We would usually bring several game plans into the game and adjust according to how the other team seemed like they wanted to play that day."

This is the trickiest part of creating a game plan. Your team is doomed if you don't have one, but even when you do, circumstances may require you to change it. The best leaders have this in mind and, like Coach Spurrier, embark on each endeavor with a firm plan based on studied preparation and, just in case, one or more backup plans.

Spurrier's Florida teams were known for their ability to audible, or change the play right before the ball was snapped in order to exploit a change in the competition's strategy. That was one of the primary ways his teams employed new game plans.

> I'm a big believer that there's a good play for just about every defense. The more often a team has good plays called, the more chances there are for big plays, so we would try to audible a little bit more than most teams. We encouraged our quarterback to do so, and sometimes we would just yell them in from the sidelines.

An audible system greatly aids the coach in employing changes in strategy during the middle of the game—especially because he is not on the field. The team is on the field, and the only people who can ensure that necessary changes are made are the team members. With an audible system already in place, the team leader (in football, the quarterback) is able to employ adjustments that were determined before the game began. To paraphrase Coach Spurrier, this allows a team to put its best foot forward every step of the way. This is the primary advantage of having backup plans.

As a player, I had no idea how detailed the planning was for our games—how many hours the coaches worked in order to prepare us for each play in the game. It really wasn't until I joined the coaching ranks at Georgetown that I began to develop a firsthand appreciation for effective planning.

During my first year of coaching as a graduate assistant at Georgetown College, one of my primary assignments was to study our opponent's game film each week and determine if there were any predictable tendencies. Most teams have them—favorite plays they like to run under certain conditions—so I would try to determine those typical plays, and then create a chart that indicated what defense we should run to stop them in those situations.

We were hosting a nationally ranked team out of Michigan by the name of Northwood Institute, and I got inside the coach's head that week. I knew how he thought and analyzed and prepared for the game, and as a result, our team was ready. During the game, they would come upon certain situations, and I would call down to the headsets on field and say, "They're gonna run a trap right." The coaches quickly signaled to the players on the field, and immediately our guys started hollering, "Watch out for the trap right! Watch out for the trap right!" This went on all afternoon. I'd notice a certain tendency and call down to say, "They're gonna run a power sweep to the left." And they'd run a power sweep to the left, and our guys would hammer them.

The opposing coach got so frustrated that he called a time-out and charged the referee to indict us. He claimed we tapped into his headset and were listening to him and his coaches discuss plays. "You guys are cheating!" he yelled. "This is unfair," he told the ref. "We want new independent headsets so they can't listen in to us and interfere with our plays!"

Well, of course, that was totally untrue. We had him, and there was nothing he could do. We went on to win the game and pull off a major upset because we were prepared to adjust our plan according to what we knew the competition might do.

An additional lesson I learned from that experience was to study the competition's tendencies in order to create a backup plan, and also to understand your own tendencies so that you never become too predictable.

Plan Thoroughly, but Remain Flexible

In an ideal world, our original game plans would succeed without incident. But as any leader with experience knows, change is inevitable. The competition changes. Markets change. Personnel change. You change. The leadership lesson to this point is simple: plan thoroughly, but prepare the team for change.

Let's talk a little more about this so it is clear.

6

Game-Day Adjustments

The team was trailing badly. The players went into the game with a solid plan but were just getting outwitted. I remember sitting in the press box looking for any adjustments that might help the team. Just before half, I noticed one on offense that would free up the running backs for days.

—COACH MULLINS

In every way you can, you find those little differences that end up being the big difference in winning the ball game.

—COACH FULMER, University of Tennessee
1998 National Champions

The following year at Georgetown College, we had to go to Michigan to play Northwood Institute on their home field. This time they weren't taking us for granted. They worked very hard to prepare, and come game time they knew us inside and out. After the first half, they were leading by two touchdowns.

At halftime we decided to totally change our approach to the game. We would run with no huddle the entire second half. We would treat all thirty minutes like a two-minute drill, as though we had only two minutes left in the game. The goal was to remain unpredictable and keep Northwood off balance and unable to make defensive adjustments.

Our plan worked off an audible system that we practiced all week so, if necessary, we could call every play from the line of scrimmage. To pull this off, we relied on a series of plays we called the "Big 5." They were a series of five plays that our guys had already memorized, and all we had to do in the huddle was say, "Big 5!" and our guys would know how to execute the plan.

With the new approach, we were able to start putting points on the board. By the fourth quarter, we had tied the game and were driving for another score. Then one of the Northwood cornerbacks came up to our wide receiver and said, "We know what your five plays are, and I know what this play is gonna be. They're gonna throw it to you on an out pattern."

He was right. That *was* the play we called; but what the cornerback didn't know is that we also had another audible between the receiver and the quarterback—it was a signal that the players used to counter something they thought the defensive backs were going to do. If they played our receivers tight on the line, we could fake an out pattern and then throw long. This is exactly what we did. Our receiver ran his out pattern, and the defensive back flew up anticipating the quick pass. Immediately our receiver turned upfield, and our quarterback hit him long for the winning touchdown.

Predictably Unpredictable

A coach has to be ready to change his game plan at any moment, and so should any leader. A mistaken notion of many leaders is that if the team just works harder, it will improve. This is not the whole story. While hard work is obviously important, if a team cannot adjust with the ebbs and flows of the game, it will achieve only inconsistent success because the game rarely remains the same.

On the other hand, when a leader has a plan but remains open to change, he keeps his team primed for success. This is typically where an effective audible system—like the one that Coach Spurrier mentioned in the last chapter—best comes into play. It prepares the team to handle changes quickly and allows the players to avoid making radical adjustments and losing momentum.

The leader who desires the best return for his team's effort must plan thoroughly—there are obvious advantages to this—but he cannot predict every step necessary to succeed. At times, the best he can do is to prepare his team to stay one step ahead of change. That's because there are many uncertainties along the path to success. College coaches understand this well. Every play in every game represents a potential wrench in their plans, an unpredictable circumstance that requires a new plan or an adjustment to the current one. What, for instance, does a coach do when his starting quarterback is injured on the first play? Or what does he do when the competition is still ahead with only two minutes left in the game? These aren't desirable circumstances, and a perfect game wouldn't include them. But if a coach is to lead his team to victory, he must have a plan for when they arise.

Ideally, a well-thought-out game plan would always go off without a hitch. But hitches unfortunately are part of the game. In general, there are three kinds that any leader might face in an effort to lead his team to victory.

Hitch #1: The Competition Changes.

Coach Bowden is known for his teams' ability to efficiently adjust to their competition's every move. Clearly the competition is gunning for—and subsequently pulling out all the stops to dethrone—a team like Florida State that is consistently ranked in the top ten. That is why it is often more difficult to remain at the top than to get there in the first place. Nevertheless, Coach Bowden seems to have learned a little something about effective game planning despite ever-changing, always gunning competition.

"You can compare it with war," he explained:

After the first bullet is fired, the whole plan might change. That's the way football is. You get a game plan for the best way to attack the competition based on what you've seen, then you go out there and you snap that ball and discover they changed completely. They anticipated and changed. Now all of a sudden what you planned to do is ineffective, and you've got to go to plan two or something else. It's the same thing defensively; you were expecting them to run the pro formation and they came out in a spread formation . . . I think, often, our plan changed in the first series of the game.

[Regardless], you have to have a plan; you have to have that first. And then you have to have an alternate plan in case something changes.

Bowden's final point is important. Every leader needs a thorough game plan first, an initial blueprint for victory, before he can be effective at making adjustments. Game-day adjustments are rarely effective if they do not, at the very least, continually exploit a team's strengths or the competition's weaknesses. If all a leader knows is how to lead his team to victory in one set of circumstances, with his team taking foreseen actions and the competition following suit, then what will happen when the circumstances change? What will happen when the competition adjusts its approach to success and is no longer predictable? If the coach has not prepared for this, he will often be grasping at straws, and the team will be frequently flailing on the field. It's a hit-or-miss approach that misses more often than it hits.

Hitch #2: The Team Changes.

Though it happens less often, the faces on a team can change in the heat of battle. In football, this typically comes about as a result of injury. In business, a team member may call in sick or have a personal matter that takes him or her from work. Regardless of how it comes about, the leader has to deal with new strengths and different weaknesses, not to mention altered team chemistry. Every one of the eight coaches acknowledged that a leader must be prepared for such changes.

For instance, what if a team's starting quarterback is injured on the first play and the second-stringer is a better passer and a slower runner than his predecessor? Wouldn't the coach be foolish to continue running a wishbone offense that requires a quick-footed quarterback and minimizes the passing game? In order for the offense to be equally effective with the new quarterback, the coach must immediately know how to utilize his passing strength and minimize his running weakness as readily as he did with his starter. If he does not, his team will suffer a drop in productivity that is likely to result in failure. The successful leader is aware of this unenviable result and takes precautions.

Hitch #3: The Climate Changes.

In football, a climate change is easily recognized. You go into a game with a passing attack that will give the competition fits—and then it begins to rain. What do you do? You can't keep throwing the ball because the receivers are having trouble making cuts and the quarterback is having trouble gripping the ball. To be successful, you have to adjust the game plan according to the change in climate. This is no different in a corporate setting.

The presentation to the big overseas client was scheduled to take place in your office next Wednesday. The company's vice president and chief marketing officer happened to be in town on other business and agreed to work your meeting into their schedule. Now, something's come up, and they have to fly home early. They would still like to meet; however, the meeting has to take place at the London office at the end of the week. And by the way, instead of just presenting to two officers of the company, they'd like you to present to their entire executive team of forty people. Big difference in climate. What needs to be done differently?

On a smaller scale, what happens when the founder of the company decides to spend half a day in the offices observing how your team is doing with the latest project? Clearly a change in climate is not something to be ignored.

Changing with Change

Ultimately game-day adjustments are best seen as microplans, alternate blueprints that take into account the varying sets of circumstances that may arise over the course of an endeavor to success. And when you consider that a team's consistent success only increases the likelihood that the competition will change the face of the game, an ability to make adjustments becomes more important as a team becomes more effective.

College coaches understand the inevitability of change as well as any leader, and that is why I felt the eight national champions would have much insight to offer on the topic. When the coaches and I talked about game planning—the subject of the last chapter—discussing game-day adjustments was unavoidable. The acknowledgment of their necessity often occurred in the same breath with the plan itself. In fact, game-day adjustments seemed to be as important as—if not more than—their game plans. Here's what I mean.

When I left the coaching ranks at Georgetown College and moved into full-time ministry, I returned on the weekends to watch the games. One weekend we were playing at home, and the team was trailing badly. The players went into the game with a solid plan but were just getting outwitted. I remember sitting in the press box looking for any adjustments that might help the team. Just before half, I noticed one on offense that would free up the running backs for days.

Since the coach and I were good friends, I made my way to the locker room during the break and stole a minute with him. I said, "Hey, Coach, let me tell you something I observed from the press box." I shared what I'd seen, and he immediately replied, "Tom, I'm gonna make those adjustments." And he did. The turnaround was amazing.

When the team made simple adjustments in the offensive blocking scheme, huge holes started opening up for the backs. The strong ground game then opened up the passing game. Methodically the team pulled closer, then even, and then ahead for good.

That day, the coach and I were reminded of the necessity of game-day adjustments. In fact, in my fifteen years of coaching and two decades of leading a church, I can honestly say I don't remember a team endeavor that didn't require at least one adjustment to the original plan. Looking back, I see that team success has always required change somewhere along the way.

The question now at hand: How does a leader initiate and execute effective game-day changes? The eight coaches' comments during our time together detailed three ingredients that answer this question. Keep in mind that these are necessary not to keep an original game plan intact, but to achieve the ultimate goal of every game plan: victory. By combining these three ingredients, your game plans will retain the necessary pliability to adjust with the inevitable changes that arise over the course of your team's endeavors.

Ingredient 1: Thorough Input

The coach is on the sidelines with his players where he should be. There is one place, however, he is not: the field of play. His perspective is limited, much like that of the CEO of a large corporation who cannot be with the team on every field call and in every client meeting. The coach *needs* to be on the field; don't get me wrong— just as the CEO needs to spend as much time as he can with his team members. But there is only so much one can learn with one set of eyes and ears.

How did the wide receiver on the far side of the field run his route on that last play? Did the center block the linebacker? The coach doesn't know either answer because he was watching the quarterback. He can observe only one thing at a time. Therefore, he must rely on the eyes and ears of others to gain enough feedback to know how and when the team should make adjustments.

Coach McCartney explained it well:

> The key to effective coaching is knowing that when you stand on the sidelines, you can't see everything. Your eyes up above are more accurate than your eyes on the sideline. There are many times when you're blocked out. What really happened? Why did that play work? Why did that play fail? You can't see it all so you need great communication. This requires people who are highly competent and skilled in seeing things from above who can then communicate in a real succinct way so that you can make decisions. Then when the players come off the field, you can zero in and say this, this, this, and this [needs to happen]. Otherwise, I've found if you ask your kids what happened out there, what they tell you will not be what you see on film next week.

In any team endeavor—especially with larger teams—it is nearly impossible for one leader to process enough information to prompt an effective game-day adjustment. He needs more than one pair of eyes and ears, and the more pairs the better. Coach McCartney's comment provides the first action a leader must take: place knowledgeable people in bird's-eye-view locations, and empower them to pass along pertinent information to you.

Is there a weakness in the competition that you'd like to verify? Is a team member better suited in another position? Is someone excelling and should be used in a more prominent role? Where is the team struggling? Succeeding? These are the kinds of questions your birds can answer for you on a regular basis, at times when you cannot see or hear all that is happening on (or in) the field. Helping these people to know what to look for and teaching them how to give concise, relevant feedback are necessary first; but once you've done this, your birds are invaluable. They help you collect the information for making quick adjustments that will keep your team in the game.

I played this role for my Georgetown friend. From my bird's-eye perch in the press box I supplied him with relevant feedback so the team could effectively adjust to the competition. I focused on one thing: what the team needed to do—or not do—in order to succeed. This kind of regular input is critical for any leader.

Ingredient 2: Quick but Poised Assessment

When I asked Coach Fulmer how he handles the changes that arise over the course of a game, he insisted,

> You cannot get yourself into a panic in those situations. We have what we call answer sheets that we carry with us to help us with issues that we've had in the past or that somebody else had that we can learn from. So we'll look at our answer sheet and have some basic things in our system that we can go to instead. This helps a coach to not get stuck somewhere. I think it's important to have poise, an answer sheet, and to remember that the game is going to be for sixty minutes. You are going to have time to make some adjustments. In no more than one or two series, you can have things corrected.

Coach Fulmer adds valuable insight to the mix. In order for a leader to determine what, if any, changes need to be made, he cannot jump to conclusions. He needs to keep his wits about him and make an educated decision. According to Fulmer, a good way to do this is to have what Tennessee called "answer sheets." These are composed before the game and provide action plans for every conceivable change that may arise over the course of the game. For instance: "Question: If the starting quarterback is injured, what do we do? Answer: Our backup quarterback has a better arm and slower feet so we will employ such and such passing plays into the offense."

Also note that the answer sheets don't provide solutions just to problems. For instance: "Question: What if it's third down and 20 or more yards to go, and the competition is running a prevent defense with seven defensive backs? Answer: Run such and such or such and such. Maybe a middle screen to the running back or a 12-yard pass to the tight end underneath the coverage." I think you get the picture. The answer sheets are there to provide precise team responses to change situations that would otherwise require more time and thought.

Unlike most leaders, the coach does not have a day, let alone a week, to make accurate assessments. He has, in most instances, a few minutes—often less than thirty seconds—to determine whether an adjustment needs to be made. If you're a business leader, consider what you would do in the following situation: you arrive at the office at 8:50 a.m. and learn that your marketing director spent the night in the ER with a severe case of food poisoning; as a result, he cannot make the 9:00 a.m. presentation to the major client you've been pursuing for six months. Do you have a response for that scenario? Now consider that a similar problem affects your 10:00 a.m., 11:00 a.m., and 1:00 p.m. meetings as well. This is the plight of coaches on a mild scale. It's fairly easy to see why answer sheets are necessary for them, but I believe they are indispensable for any leader.

In sum, answer sheets are valuable because they inject immediate reasoning into an otherwise stressful situation. They provide advanced insight—the thinking has already been done before the game began—and they allow the leader to make well-informed decisions in a highly efficient manner. Any leader would be wise to use a similar system before sending his team onto the field.

Then there is one more ingredient for making effective game-day adjustments. Namely, applying the input you've received and the assessments you've made to the team's efforts.

Ingredient 3: Effective Execution

"What is most important," advised Coach Stoops, "is making sure the players understand what is happening to them and what we want to do about it. It does no good as a coach if you know what you want to do and you don't relay the information. So we do our best to make sure our players fully understand what's happening to them and how we want to deal with it . . . Coaches are constantly conferencing on the phone, analyzing how the other team is attacking us and what we need to do and how we need to adjust; and then when the players come off the field, we make sure they have that information and give them our plan for the next series."

Coach Stoops is dead-on. It does no good to have thorough input and poised assessment if you fail to apply the necessary adjustments on the field. Getting the players involved is the final step. There are a number of ways to do this, but every champion coach employs a system that involves relaying the necessary adjustments to team leaders who then relay the adjustments to the rest of the team. The premise of using the system is having a team leader with a good understanding of the team's makeup and capabilities so that the explanation he requires is not drawn out and time-consuming.

In essence, the team leader—in football, typically the quarterback—should require little explanation in order to apply the adjustments on the field. To this end, Coaches Osborne and Spurrier spent a lot of time with their quarterbacks empowering them to make adjustment decisions on their own throughout the game. "We gave them free rein," explained Osborne. "I coached the quarterback, and we spent a lot of time on audibles—I gave them an audible sheet. We did a lot of either/or. You know, [run] one option or another option . . . As time went on . . . we would [get to the point where] we could call every play from the line of scrimmage."

Spurrier relied on a similar system of empowerment to apply necessary adjustments: "I tried to coach our quarterback to audible a little more than most teams . . . We encouraged our quarterbacks to do so."

The value of an audible system—as we touched on last chapter—is its efficiency, but there is more. When the quarterback, or any team leader, is trained to instinctively employ necessary game-day adjustments, there is less danger of decelerating momentum or dampening morale. In short, the team is able to seamlessly advance toward victory. This strategy does not take the coach out of the equation; it merely expands and expedites his leadership capacity. Leaders who employ a similar system of empowerment enjoy the same advantages. My story illustrates this point.

When I came to Florida to be a college athletic director, we placed our son into a high school called the Benjamin School. The school started its first football program that year, and the A.D., Mickey Neal, was a good friend of mine who asked me to help with the new team in the afternoons. I was thrilled to agree because it gave me the opportunity to be a part of coaching my son. Little did we know that year would be special in more ways than one.

One challenge with a new program is that typically every team you play has superior talent or, at the very least, more seasoned talent. We decided to address this challenge head-on by teaching the team an audible system that would allow us to outthink our opponents. In effect, we hoped that doing this would keep our games on an intellectual level where we felt we had an advantage.

In unexpected fashion, the plan worked from day one. The guys on the team were very bright and learned the system quickly and effectively. As a result, they were able to continually exploit their opponents' weaknesses each week. We got on a roll, and in the end, though we were physically outmatched in every game, we won our way to the state championship in our inaugural year.

The Surest Path

Ultimately adjusting to the changes that arise in a game is all about taking the surest path to victory. Of course, your team will still face unforeseen circumstances now and then, but the greatest leaders take the time to spoil the effects of as many surprises as they can. And they learn more as they go.

I've mentioned before that I'm a believer that great leadership requires a level of intuition, but I also believe that no leader should rely on it when it's unnecessary. If you can prepare your team ahead of time for potential setbacks, you should. Why wouldn't you?

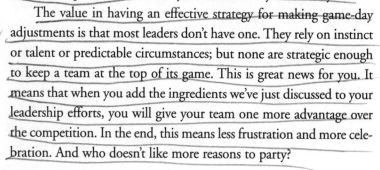

The value in having an effective strategy for making game-day adjustments is that most leaders don't have one. They rely on instinct or talent or predictable circumstances; but none are strategic enough to keep a team at the top of its game. This is great news for you. It means that when you add the ingredients we've just discussed to your leadership efforts, you will give your team one more advantage over the competition. In the end, this means less frustration and more celebration. And who doesn't like more reasons to party?

7

Celebration

I don't care how badly you want something; you've got to get everybody else to want it as badly as you do, and the only way you can do that is to celebrate. You've got to jump up and down and be happy for each other.

—COACH MCCARTNEY, University of Colorado
1990 National Champions

I can remember some of the locker rooms after many accomplished championships where it was very emotional because there is usually a lot of closeness between the players and coaches. I certainly didn't want to pour cold water on that.

—COACH OSBORNE, University of Nebraska
1994, 1995, and 1997 National Champions

When I was coaching at Texas A&M," Coach Stallings began, "we beat LSU in Baton Rouge. Now we didn't play all that well, but we did win the game. Afterward, I happened to be walking by one of the coach's offices and heard him coming down on a player so hard. Now listen, if you can't enjoy the win, you got a little bit of a problem. If you can't find something good out of a win, then you're in the wrong business. You know, I fired the guy. I said, 'Look, now we might not have played great on every play, and I understand that, but, hey, we won the game.'

"See, the fun is in the winning. If you can't let any fun be in the winning, then where is the fun? It's not in the practice. It's not in making the trip. It's not always in the playing. The fun is in the winning, and if you can't enjoy a win, then as far as I'm concerned, you're in the wrong business. I mean, if I can't get high there, or if the team can't get high on that, then, brother, we got a problem."

The Fun Is in the Winning

I loved hearing that story from the mouth of Coach Stallings, a leader known for his firmness and forthrightness. His story was also timely as our interview was my last with the coaches, and it seemed to sum up the feeling of all eight. Namely, that authentic celebration is an essential component of team leadership.

A common misconception among young coaches is that a "one game at a time" mentality necessitates downplaying every win until the big one, the championship. This is a naïve strategy, and it is dangerous. I played for a coach who used this approach. He preached the creed that celebration was excessive and unnecessary until we won the championship game. He'd come into the locker room after a win while we were slapping hands and carrying on, and he'd tell us to calm down, it wasn't time to celebrate yet—we needed to forget about the win and focus on the next game. He wouldn't let us celebrate for even five minutes, and it never felt right—sort of like a parent telling you not to smile on your birthday.

If a team is not allowed to celebrate each victory, not only are the individuals' spirits dampened at a time when they should be soaring, but their efforts are never validated or recognized. If the routine continues, the team may start to ask, "What's the point?"

Sure, it's important to keep a team focused on the big goal, yet if a team's expectations for one step are met but quickly overlooked, the players' energy and excitement for the next step will shrink. The central problem is that you can't very well get them excited to take the second step if you never acknowledged that they took the first step successfully.

Coach McCartney recognized that a "don't celebrate until the championship" mentality is ultimately grounded in innocent ambition, and he addressed its chief problem from that perspective: "I don't care how badly you [the coach] want something; you've got to get everybody else to want it as badly as you do, and the only way you can do that is to celebrate. You've got to celebrate when individuals reach goals. You've got to celebrate when somebody does something significant. You've got to jump up and down and be happy for each other . . . You have to acknowledge their contribution."

McCartney's staff and players regarded him as a great encourager. He was always making an extra effort to recognize the smaller successes of team members. In fact, he came to rely on their successes as a gauge of his own success. When I asked him about this, he was humble in his answer. "I never was a great coach," he insisted, "but I learned . . . to delegate and empower. I was never really a great coach, but I had good people around me and they were able to become all they could be because I gave them the opportunity."

The lesson thus far is that victory should never be discounted. It should be shared and celebrated.

The value of this approach on the team level is that what gets celebrated takes emotional priority in the hearts of the team members. In other words, because they enjoy the feeling of victory, they want to experience it again—so much so that at times we say they can "smell" victory.

On the individual level, when an accomplishment is celebrated, the team member is validated, his effort is noted as being worthwhile, and he leaves the celebration more motivated to excel. This doesn't indicate that an individual has selfish motives; it indicates that as people, we are motivated by more than hope and promise. We are *also* motivated by gratification and gratitude. Celebration is the leader's vehicle for passing them out.

Why We Celebrate

Strategic celebration meets five objectives. We'll touch on them briefly before we ask the coaches how they meet these objectives most effectively.

Objective #1: Celebration Acknowledges Accomplished Goals.

Celebration affirms that expectations were met and lays the groundwork for setting new expectations. This begins, always, with an acknowledgment of good teamwork because it is the one staple ingredient in victory—like the sugar in any great dessert. After acknowledging good teamwork, celebration affirms the meeting of individual goals that helped the team reach its corporate goal.

Objective #2: Celebration Validates the Effort Needed to Achieve Victory.

To teach a team what it takes to succeed, always celebrate the efforts of the members to provide them with a frame of reference for future endeavors. If a leader does not provide the team with this, he will often curb the enthusiasm for the next challenge—if there is nothing fulfilling about victory, then there is little reason to pursue it wholeheartedly. A leader must validate a team's hard work if he desires it to continue.

Objective #3: Celebration Motivates the Team to Try Harder.

Often, a team's first success isn't a result of the members' best effort. It merely shows them what they can accomplish when they apply themselves to the task of winning. But typically once a team tastes victory, the participants find that they can and will work harder to taste it again.

Objective #4: Celebration Improves Attitudes.

I think we all understand this objective. In a party atmosphere, everybody's spirit is lifted; and the more parties you have, the better your team tends to feel. It's what Coach Stallings was talking about when he said, "The fun is in the winning."

Objective #5: Celebration Attracts New Team Members.

Again, there's nothing complicated about this. People want to be part of something fun, something fulfilling, something successful. Celebrations show outsiders that being a part of your team is where it's at.

When I coached high school football, we always held school-wide pep rallies to get the students excited before the big games. We made it a point to highlight the personal achievements of the players on our team. We had a player of the week, a lineman of the week, a receiver of the week, and so on. Following these rallies, several kids who had been in the stands always approached the coaching staff about joining the team. We had never had much response from guys asking to try out for the team until we instituted pep rallies with the student body. After sharing our victories with others, the boys looking on wanted to be a part of what we had going.

The Secrets of Strategic Celebration

It feels a little weird to talk about celebration from a strategic standpoint. After all, having fun shouldn't require a plan. All of the coaches agreed with this. However, they also agreed that the game must go on.

Coach Osborne explained it this way:

> I can remember some of the locker rooms after many accomplished championships where it was very emotional because there is usually a lot of closeness between the players and coaches. I certainly didn't want to pour cold water on that. But sometimes you'll see a team win a big game and then lose the next week because

they celebrated heavily for three or four days. So when we came out to practice on Monday, we were ready to move on to the next team.

A celebration strategy should not take from its spontaneous nature. A leader has to be careful about this. Yet all celebrations must come to an end if the big goal is to be reached. This is Osborne's point. A win is worthy of celebration; but until the championship is won, celebration must adhere to the task of advancing the team closer to its goal. The general purpose of a strategy, then, is to determine when, where, and how long it is appropriate. These are the questions I put to the eight coaches, and their answers give us four steps for using strategic celebration in our own team leadership endeavors.

Step 1: Be Clear About What Constitutes a Celebration.

For college coaches, one part of this is easy. Winning a game constitutes a celebration. Similarly, there are wins for your team that clearly call for celebration. Securing a big account, for instance. Meeting a fund-raising goal. Designing a stellar campaign. Becoming tops in sales in your industry. These are evident reasons to party, and most leaders know them without thinking. However, the other component of this step is more subjective and requires good intuition. That's because it involves determining which individual efforts also call for celebration.

To address this correctly, the team must have clear-cut goals. They are the hinge for deciphering what efforts are celebration-worthy.

When a leader—with the help of his team—lays out clear-cut goals for the group and each individual, everyone understands when a celebration is in order. Obviously the key here is to set realistic goals that truly require special effort. But keep in mind, too, that these need not be major milestones. Give attention to small goals as well.

For instance, a championship coach may not make throwing one touchdown a game a goal for his quarterback (the goal would be met nearly every week and lose its significance). The coach might instead set an individual goal for his quarterback to pass for 300 yards in a game or throw three touchdowns. These are feasible goals that, when reached, will give the team a solid chance of winning the game. The primary criterion of an individual goal is that meeting it should greatly increase the team's chances for victory. If this is true of a goal, then a celebration is in order when it is met. If this is not necessarily true of an individual goal, then a new or higher goal should be reached before a celebration is fitting.

Each of the eight coaches approached celebrating individual accomplishments in similar fashion by asking their players to set personal goals and then helping them to hone the goals (and at times set them higher) to best suit the overall efforts of the team. This way, expectations were always clear, and there was little room for players feeling overlooked.

Coach Fulmer explained how this celebratory foundation plays out—first, on a team level, and second, on an individual level—with his Volunteers: "Immediately after [winning] a game, we honor each other and celebrate together. We have a little song that we always sing together. Then, on Mondays when we come back together to watch the film, we spend ten minutes recognizing each other's accomplishments." His example is a good one to follow as it keeps the individual celebrations very team-oriented.

We employ a similar approach at our church. Every Tuesday in our staff meeting we set aside the first thirty minutes to celebrate individual and department victories. This time recognizes the team members whose efforts advanced the church's mission and therefore added value to us all.

To take this first step, verify that the people on your team are set up with victory-enhancing goals, and then make it a habit to regularly celebrate your team victories and the individual accomplishments that help usher them in.

Step 2: Keep It Personal, Not Pretentious.

More recently in football, coaches have had to come to terms with their stance on field celebrations. What is permissible, and what is not? Is it okay for a player to spike the ball or do a dance in the end zone? Where is the line drawn? What are the guidelines for celebration? There were two different approaches to this among the eight coaches, characterized by the responses of Coaches Stallings and Stoops to the celebration questions.

Coach Stoops is more inclined to encourage celebration on the field. "It creates excitement," he said, "and the game is played with a lot of excitement, so we encourage it . . . as long as we don't get a penalty."

His point is well made. Any team endeavor—especially a college football game—requires a high level of intensity, and to discourage that can be a detriment. However, there is also danger in being too lax. Coach Stallings was certain to avoid this. While he loved celebrating with his teams, he confessed that he felt it should be reserved for the locker room. "I loved celebrating when the game was over," he explained, "but always in the privacy of the dressing room. I wasn't into all that showboating out on the field."

While it seems that the two hold opposing views, they actually represent two sides of the same coin. On one side of the coin, celebration should fuel enthusiasm, and a wise leader will not hinder it. On the other side, celebration is for the team's sake, to promote unity and excitement among teammates, not for the purpose of gloating or showboating or turning the spotlight on an individual. The key is promoting both definitions to the team.

Coach Stoops concluded his explanation this way: "We want the team to celebrate together as much as possible, to show enthusiasm and excitement and share it with one another. [But] we tell them to never celebrate alone, never celebrate to the crowd by yourself but only around your teammates . . . We don't want them to be foolish about it."

In similar fashion, it's important for you to define the details of appropriate celebration. In the first step, you help your team understand when to celebrate. In this step, say the coaches, you teach them why to celebrate.

You don't need to state the obvious. Your goal is to help the team understand the purpose of celebration—specifically, that it is first a private matter and, second, an act designed to knit them closer together. By contrast, it is not for the purpose of gloating to the competition or spotlighting individuals. A leader who helps the team understand these essential definitions will help ensure that celebration never loses its charm.

Step 3: Determine When to Move On.

Every one of the coaches agreed on this step, primarily because their teams cannot over-celebrate a win when the next challenge is waiting in the wings, just six days later. Coach Spurrier epitomized the group's insight on this matter:

> We didn't over-celebrate our victories. We tried to teach our players that we would enjoy the victory that day and night, but the next morning when we got up, we would start focusing on the next opponent. We felt like the real celebration would be after the last game of the season, and hopefully that would be after some kind of championship—a bowl game or the national championship.
>
> One of the nicest things written about our team was in 1996 when we played at Knoxville. They enlarged their stadium up to 110,000, and they were billing it as the largest crowd in

the history of Tennessee football, and by the second quarter we had them thirty-five to nothing. It was just one of those games; they turned it over, and we scored on our first five possessions and then held on to win. After the game, one of the sports writers said for a big crowd and a big game, it was no big deal to the Gators. He described our locker room as typical: one of high fives and hugging and slapping. It was just another game at the ballpark for the Gators. That was a nice compliment because it was early in the season and not time to celebrate big yet. So we enjoyed the victory and went on to have a huge season.

For a football team on the road to the championship, the next step begins almost immediately. This doesn't mean a team should forgo celebrating well. It does mean that facing and meeting the next challenge requires enough discipline to put the party hats down and get back to business when it's time.

For every championship coach, this took on the form of a twenty-four-hour rule; celebration was encouraged wholeheartedly following a victory for twenty-four hours, but once that time was up, the players were expected to start preparing for the next challenge: mentally, emotionally, and physically. "I do like for them to enjoy the victories," explained Coach Bowden. "They deserve to enjoy them. However, if we play on a Saturday, that joy or any kind of expression of that joy is usually over by Sunday night. [I'd tell them], 'Enjoy yourself. You won the game. Hold your chest up high. But Monday we're starting all over again.'"

Coach Stoops agreed: "We allow them to enjoy the victory until it is time to go back to work. We give them Sundays to celebrate, and we're back to work on Monday."

Leaders of any size team can benefit from this approach. Often it's easy to allow the celebration of a victory to linger because it acts as a feel-good drug. Following a victory, the team remains in good spirits, and everyone gets along. However, the feelings represent a false high if the team is only putting off engaging the next task at hand.

The best way to avoid this, even if the next task is not a big one, is to employ a similar rule for all celebrations that are not the *big* celebration. If you're a business leader, you may want to play with the length of time you allow yourself and the team to celebrate victories, all according to the next challenge. If a goal is met on Friday, for instance, you may want to employ a forty-eight-hour rule that encourages the team to celebrate from Friday night to Sunday night and then come back on Monday with clear minds ready to engage the next challenge. If it's a midweek celebration, you may want to employ a half-day rule that indicates the team can celebrate the second half of the workday but is expected to reengage the next challenge once the individuals return to the office the following morning. I could offer more examples, but I think you get the picture. Ultimately it's critical to get the team to see the value in this step—namely, that its aim is not to dampen the celebrations or lessen the accomplishments, but to allow the team to preserve energies and enthusiasm for pursuing the big goal: the championship.

Step 4: Determine When to Blow It Out.

Whether it's at the end of the championship game or the end of a long and victorious campaign, the leader must know when it's time to let loose and let the good times roll. The leader can go overboard here. It is his time to show with certainty the value he places on and the appreciation he has for his team. Each coach was adamant about this. When the big game is won, it's time to blow it out. It's the team's time to feel special.

There are many ways a leader can do this. Coach Spurrier mentioned one way he helped his teams immortalize the memory of their big wins: "One thing that our team started doing after winning a championship is taking team pictures. We've done this with all our conference championships starting at Duke in 1989 and seven at Florida. Then for the national [championship], we took a team picture with uniforms underneath the scoreboard after the game. That was something that the players could get a copy of and take with them the rest of their lives."

That is just one of the many ways a leader can commemorate the team's big victory and make the celebration extra special. When our church moved into a new $20 million facility a few years ago, we still had a $5 million debt on it, and I wanted us to work aggressively to reduce that debt so we could invest our money into ministry and missions. We set a goal and challenged our church family.

Within three months, the congregation rallied together monthly commitments that would pay off the remainder of the debt in one year. Once we received news of the goal, we immediately planned a celebration, and we called it the Freedom Bowl.

We designed our weekend services to resemble a pep rally for a football game. Our choir dressed up with signs that read, "Go! Fight! Win!" and "We're #1!" Our stage was converted to a football field and stadium, complete with authentic goal posts. I donned a football uniform that read "Freedom Bowl" on the jersey with my old number, 42, beneath it. Then to kick it off, one of our guys introduced the celebration over the loudspeaker. Simultaneously smoke billowed from the sides of the stage, and I came running from the back of the church and down the aisle through our people, high-fiving everyone I passed. When I reached the stage, everyone was going crazy. People started throwing Nerf footballs stamped with "Freedom Bowl" into the audience. We celebrated long and big that day because we felt the church made a big sacrifice and accomplished something extraordinary.

People still remember that celebration. As a matter of fact, several people were visiting that day and got so caught up in the enthusiasm and passion and camaraderie that they stayed with us and are now members in our church.

Celebrate Often

The Freedom Bowl reminded me of the great value that celebration holds for a team. But remember that a leader doesn't always have to blow it out in order to validate the team's efforts and keep spirits high. In fact, often the small celebrations keep us going from week to week.

On one of my high school teams in Florida, we had a kid who went by the nickname "Dirty Mac." The way he earned the name is quite interesting. The "Dirty" part fell on him because he didn't like to take showers after practice. We had to force him in there. The other half of his name arose as a result of one of our methods of weekly celebration.

To reward special efforts in our practices and games, we often gave away coupons for free food, which the guys liked. Sometimes a guy would come in from the practice field where he worked hard and gave his all, and even though he might not have been a starter on the team, we would find a way to celebrate his accomplishment. This included presenting him with a Big Mac Award, a coupon for a free Big Mac.

Dirty Mac was a talented offensive lineman who often earned these awards. Every time we scored a touchdown over his hole, every time he knocked a defensive lineman on his back, every time he successfully executed a big play, the team celebrated, and he received his coupons. It quickly became something the team looked forward to each week because Dirty Mac was known to stockpile his coupons, even bartering with teammates for more, and then head to McDonald's and eat four in one sitting. Thus he became known as Dirty Mac, the teammate who liked to be dirty and loved to eat Big Macs.

That year his ongoing story made our small celebrations enormously fun and memorable. So memorable, in fact, that the guys on the team still affectionately call him Dirty Mac today, now a grown man in his late forties.

I tell you that story because it illustrates the effect of genuine celebration. As leaders, we need to find ways to reward success both big and small. We need to know when to blow it out and go crazy, and we also need to know when to pause if only for a few minutes and say, "Look at the job Dirty Mac did!"

It's a grave mistake to get too busy and pass over the little victories. A leader has to learn to push the pause button now and then and initiate celebration. There are always reasons to celebrate.

When I was a coach, my teams certainly had big goals that required great commitment and a lot of consistent hard work; but we also set intermediate goals so we had reason to celebrate often. We celebrated attitude, cooperation, teamwork, excellence, and perseverance. And the things we regularly affirmed were the things we emulated most.

Section
II

Coaching Insights
for Ministry Leaders

8

Applying the
Coaching Principles in Ministry

The principles that help a coach lead a football team to victory are the very same principles a pastor can use to lead his church staff to accomplish what God has set before them. Sure, there are differences. One deals in the realm of sports and the other in the realm of the spirit, but both are lively adventures steeped in passion, zeal, and camaraderie.
—COACH MULLINS

For the past twenty-one years, I have intuitively used coaching principles to lead Christ Fellowship Church in Palm Beach County, Florida. Since 1984, I have recruited, motivated, sustained momentum and morale, planned, made adjustments, and celebrated with my church team through the mind and heart of a football coach; and we've grown steadily in both size and spirit. There are many good reasons for this, including the encouragement and support of my family, but foremost is the hand of God on our efforts. Next to His blessings, the most comprehensive reason for our accomplishments is coaching: namely, the application of the leadership lessons it taught me during my fifteen years in the high school and college ranks. I'll explain why I believe this has worked so well.

There is an obvious parallel between coaching an amateur football team and leading a church. Both are about leading a team of volunteers. High school and college football players are not paid for their efforts. Our staff at Christ Fellowship has always consisted of many more volunteers than paid staff. The ratio varies from week to week, but it generally hovers around ten to one. A similar ratio holds true in most churches in America, most of which don't retain the budget to support more than a half dozen full-timers and a couple of part-timers, if any. Facing the challenge of leading a growing ministry with a staff that primarily consists of volunteers can seem like a daunting task, but to a coach, it's just another day on the job.

The principles that help a coach lead a football team to victory are the very same principles a pastor can use to lead his church staff to accomplish what God has set before them. Sure, there are differences. One deals in the realm of sports and the other in the realm of the spirit, but both are lively adventures steeped in passion, zeal, and camaraderie. One defines success by statistics and rankings. The other, by lives changed. But regardless of the goal, I've found that team members in either scenario are moved in much the same way.

In this chapter, I'd like to take you on a stroll with me through the halls and hearts of Christ Fellowship Church to help you see how these coaching principles we've been discussing are applied in ministry—we've used them as a small church of one hundred and every step of the way to the large church we are today. Since we've already delved deep into the core of each coaching principle in the previous chapters, this chapter will deal strictly with ministry applications for all seven principles.

By observing our examples of coaching techniques at work, you can take home a few more tools for improving your church's ability to work in hand with God to spread His love abroad. Ultimately, that's what we're all after.

Let's begin our stroll where the book began, with recruiting.

Recruiting: Growing God's Team

In talking with various church staffs over the years, I've repeatedly heard the notion that ministry leaders have to wait for a bigger payroll in order to really get things accomplished in and through a church. This is clearly a misunderstanding; most churches would probably go under without the support and work of volunteers.

Where recruiting is concerned, if a ministry leader waits for more budget money to fill gaps in the team, growth will be slow and influence sparing. To grow a ministry, a leader needs a staff, yes, but a leader also has to focus efforts on maintaining a steady influx of volunteers who are readily trained to add value when and where it is needed. There are four habits that help us accomplish this each year at Christ Fellowship.

Habit 1: We Make Recruiting a Team Effort.

In the same way that coaches get their players involved in recruiting, our ministry leaders are encouraged to maintain a recruiting eye for people who could add value to that particular ministry's effort. Doing this keeps recruiting on a team level and takes the burden off any one person's shoulders. Furthermore, ministry leaders who are passionately committed are effective at recruiting others.

Habit 2: We Take the First Step.

Like coaches, we are always building relationships. We've employed a variety of ways to welcome and acclimate our first-time visitors over the years. We offer Welcome Receptions following services where visitors can meet and interact with our pastoral staff. After they visit, we call to invite them to join us again and offer them the opportunity to attend a class that introduces them to our staff and gives an explanation of the church's history, vision, and mission. We have used a special event called the Connections Luncheon following the services, where a meal is served, and each table is hosted by one of our pastors. This gives new members an opportunity to meet our staff on a personal level and ask any questions they may have.

Habit 3: We Present Numerous Opportunities for Involvement.

Many times, a recruit won't commit to a college until he knows where he fits into the offensive or defensive scheme. We understand this, and so twice a year Christ Fellowship holds a large ministry fair. All the lobbies of the church are lined with displays and active leaders of every ministry we offer. These displays serve two purposes: they allow potential recruits to determine where they might fit, and they give current members a chance to learn more about the mission of the church. Each year, our ministry fairs add more than one thousand new members to the team. I should also mention that we give the team open permission to change volunteer areas in order to better suit needs in the church body and the community. We encourage our people to volunteer in their area of passion, which sometimes means opening a new door of opportunity.

Habit 4: We Publicly Reiterate the Value of the Team.

Every year, I spend several weeks teaching a series on what it means to be involved in Christ Fellowship. In this, I reiterate our mission to the people in our city and reemphasize the accomplishments that cannot be realized without help.

One of the most important tenets of recruiting for ministry is making sure the team understands how invaluable it is. This is the umbrella of all that we do. Each of our habits is in one way connected to conveying the importance we place on the team of people that help Christ Fellowship accomplish our many missions. Last Thanksgiving is one example.

To help serve meals to fifteen thousand people in the Palm Beach community, we needed the help of hundreds of volunteers. The event was a huge success, and I made a point the following Sunday, during each service, to publicly praise the team of people. In the presence of the congregation, I asked all involved in the Thanksgiving event to stand. I praised their efforts and made sure they knew how critical their involvement was in meeting our goal. And before I let them take a seat, I led the congregation in giving them a huge round of applause. Not only did this convey to our team that we valued them, but it also made clear to future recruits that being a part of Christ Fellowship is a privilege and a pleasure.

Motivation: Passing on the Passion

I often confess to our congregation that I left coaching football in order to coach the greatest people in the world—and I mean it. I am passionate about our mission at Christ Fellowship, and one of the primary ways that we initiate new team members is by clearly laying that out for them. I want them to know what we are excited about so they can share in the enthusiasm. This process begins during recruiting and continues throughout a team member's tenure. It allows each member to insert himself into the big picture and ignites his passion to jump right in. Though it sounds simple, reiterating and redefining our mission proves to be our most effective motivational strategy. There are five principles we rely on to carry this out.

Principle 1: Passion Starts in the Pulpit.

As the senior pastor, I have the job of making sure that our team is empowered and impassioned to carry out our mission of love to our region of the country. That means two things. First, my life must embody the mission. I cannot impart what I do not possess; therefore, I must believe in what Christ Fellowship stands for, and I must live it out. Second, I must instruct my leadership team to do the same. By my example and words, I have to empower and encourage them to love people not just on Sundays, but throughout the week. Doing this from the pulpit and in our meetings constantly reminds them of the inherent value of what we do.

Principle 2: Affirmation Is Contagious.

In the same way that a coach must spread the praise around, I keep the Christ Fellowship team motivated by affirming the individual achievements regularly. In Chapter 7, "Celebration," I mentioned how we take at least thirty minutes in our weekly staff meeting to applaud the special efforts of team members. This is part of it. To add affirmation, I take frequent walks through our offices and spend a few moments with team members who are available.

I also make an effort to get around campus before and after weekend services to talk to our volunteers. I thank them for greeting our church family with genuine enthusiasm, for caring for our kids with love, and for parking cars with patience. It's important to affirm and validate them in and out of the pulpit.

Occasionally there is time only for a hello and a quick thank-you, but done consistently over time, this act keeps our teammates motivated by reminding them that they are needed to fulfill our mission.

Principle 3: Responsibility Empowers.

A ball player never knows when the coach may call on him to come through for the team. In much the same way, I make a point to randomly include team members at various levels in decision-making processes where I rely on their expertise to make significant decisions. This regular heightening of responsibility acts as a motivating force because it requires each team member to bring his best to the table every day.

I've also found that after you agree on the parameters of a task, it's best to release team members to implement it in their own creative way. This approach encourages ownership and adds longevity to the team.

Principle 4: What Gets Rewarded Gets Repeated.

When a coach rewards players who carry out key assignments with excellence, he encourages the players to place high priority on the assignment, thus helping them recall and repeat it readily. I model this principle at Christ Fellowship by setting aside budget money in each department for volunteer and paid staff appreciation. We reward not only with words, but also with meaningful gifts.

Principle 5: Natural Dynamics Provide Great Launching Points.

As a coach, you learn to stay with a play or a strategy that's working in a game. This gives the team confidence and allows the players to take big strides down the field and put points on the board very quickly. At Christ Fellowship, we rely on the same principle when launching new ministries or attempting to grow existing ones. For instance, one year we really promoted an activity for the youth at our church and in the community, and fifteen hundred students showed up. Rather than trying to reinvent the wheel, we piggybacked on the enthusiasm from that event the following year. Two thousand showed up the second year.

There's nothing ingenious about this last principle, but many ministry leaders miss it. In an effort to remain innovating and appealing, they tend toward introducing new ministries instead of utilizing ones that are already well in place and thriving. The motivating force is twofold: first, people are less excited about change than they are about tradition, and second, momentum is much easier to sustain with existing forces.

Momentum: Maintaining God's Pace

Maintaining momentum doesn't mean that ministry teams should no longer strive to improve. In fact, expansion is the key to momentum in ministry. There are two ways to view expansion: first, you can see it as outward growth moving inward, or second, you can see it as inward growth moving outward. The latter is more correct.

In other words, to sustain momentum as a ministry leader, you should have the goal of growing the individual first; then outward influence will flourish. At Christ Fellowship, this is our momentum strategy, and we break it down into four steps.

Step 1: Meet Felt Needs First.

It's easy to make the mistake of assuming the community's needs and then initiating ministries according to those assumptions. At our church, we decided this approach wasn't very effective if we were interested in ministering to people for the long haul. Instead we now ask our community for its needs through surveys and ongoing conversation. We receive clear answers and create ministries in keeping with those discoveries. In addition, we consider what ministries are already taking place informally that would benefit from more intentional planning and involvement. These actions give us steadfast influence with the people in our areas. This is a good example of positive momentum in ministry.

Step 2: Maintain a Positive Environment.

I know churches that have made a public spectacle of people they don't agree with or with whom they've had problems—even people in the church. I don't believe this is any way to sustain positive momentum.

As a coach, I never tried to make players a public spectacle. I had seen how that could cut into a team's morale and hinder its progress. At Christ Fellowship, we subscribe to the same philosophy. We deal with our problems behind closed doors and remain upbeat and positive. We never focus on what's wrong; we work on it privately and always communicate the positive side of things publicly. This is not an attempt to appear as though we don't have problems; we just don't believe our problems and issues should bog us down and spoil the environment we create for others.

Step 3: Celebrate Often.

Chapter 7 illustrated that celebration helps keep spirits high and therefore sustains momentum. This principle is obvious on the football field but sometimes taken for granted in ministry.

Ministry leaders often expect that where God is involved, celebration is built in—church people are always "rejoicing in spirit," and there is little need to make a big deal of things. This is not the case. While most ministry team members do rejoice on their own for the team's victories, physical celebration is never excessive. In fact, I believe it is necessary to validate the ministry team's efforts—even the small ones—in order to boost our momentum for the next series of tasks.

Step 4: Remain Sensitive to the Timing of Change.

A coach must know when change is timely and when it can backfire. For instance, if a quarterback is not quite getting the job done for a team, how many more games does the coach wait until he puts in the backup? We see examples every year. If the coach waits too long, the team struggles to regain momentum. If he inserts the quarterback too early, the confidence of the team may be shattered—maybe the players really believed in the first-stringer and felt he could turn it around. Often there's a tiny window for implementing change, and a great coach knows when it opens.

About four years ago, I started to notice that my ministry team was beginning to wear thin from the stress of five weekend services. It became an issue I needed to address in a timely manner. The bottom line is that we needed to move to a new facility to disperse the growing congregation better. But I knew if I waited too long, I would burn out some valuable team members, maybe lose them for good. If I initiated the move too soon, without thinking the details through, it could prove to be a big mess and take months to get back in stride. I sat down with the team, and over several meetings and with much prayer we determined the right place and right time to move. As a result of thorough planning on the front end—and involving the team in the process—the move went smoothly and the church never broke stride.

Where ministry is concerned, momentum is a little more than what you see on the outside. If the team and the people you are ministering to are not in stride and the leader is not pacing with God, momentum will be short-lived. The keys for maintaining momentum in ministry are twofold and sum up the steps we take at Christ Fellowship: walk closely with God, and grow people first.

Morale: Promoting Unity and Teamwork

Though it's easier at Christ Fellowship than it was on a football field, keeping the team's spirits high is still a major priority. In fact, we rely on high morale in ministry today more than we ever have since volunteers make up the majority of our team.

Of course, there are personal and spiritual reasons people want to be a part of a ministry team, but as the leader, you cannot take this for granted. Not only is there a very real enemy seeking to destroy everything your team sets its heart to, people are still people, and they need to be encouraged and validated on a regular basis. This is why you need to explain what you want *for* your people before you explain what you want *from* them.

Maintaining morale is so important, in fact, that it permeates two of our written core values:

> *Committed to Teamwork: Only by working together as a team will we fulfill all that God has destined for us. Each team member brings a unique talent, background, and experience, which*

jointly fits together to establish and complete the mission God has given us.

Rooted in Unity: It is imperative to keep in one mind and one accord. Though we all have different abilities and come from various backgrounds, we recognize the importance of working together. As a family, we believe in each other and look for ways to support one another.

At Christ Fellowship, we employ four specific strategies for acting out these two core values, thus ensuring that morale remains high.

Approach 1: The Teammates Pray Together.

Prayer is a top priority. We launch every endeavor with prayer and bathe every decision in prayer. Each Tuesday morning, the staff begins the day with prayer to unite our hearts and our spirits on the important issues at church and in each other's homes. In short, prayer has a central place in all our ministries. We cover every service with prayer; we have partners around the world praying specifically for us; we schedule prayer walks around the campus and conduct meetings for the explicit purpose of praying for God's direction in our day-to-day efforts.

Approach 2: The Team Shares Stories.

One day a week, we set aside a portion of the morning to open the floor to any staff member who wants to share stories of personal or corporate victory. The obvious advantage of this time is the deeper level of intimacy we achieve by knowing more about one another. The less-known advantage is that this time knits our lives together into one bigger story, much like Coach Fulmer's '98 Volunteers and the story of Moses and the promised land. By sharing personal stories and new corporate perspectives, we collectively pen a new chapter in the church's story each week.

Approach 3: We Divide the Larger Team into Smaller Groups.

The purpose of this approach is to avoid leaving anyone out of the story. Because our church is growing rapidly, the likelihood that team members will get lost in the shuffle also grows. Dividing the team into smaller groups that meet more frequently gives each team member a chance to draw closer to the heart of the team and its mission.

A football coach divides his team into smaller positional groups for the same reason. Not only does this allow the team to grow more readily on an individual basis, but it draws the players closer together and allows them to identify themselves with the team. This is why we're always hearing of names for certain groups on football teams. In the '60s there were the Vikings, and then there were the "Purple People Eaters." In the '70s there were the Steelers, and then there was the "Iron Curtain." In the '80s there were the Redskins, and then there were the "Hogs" and the "Smurfs." Smaller groups don't divide the team as long as the mission of the larger group is being furthered.

At Christ Fellowship, we have a program to meet the needs of people who are battling addictions. We have a ministry to single mothers. We also have a ministry to the elderly. We have no molds for the way ministry should happen except that it should allow us to love people and meet needs. We find that with these smaller teams, people are able to connect on a deeper level, which allows them to keep each other's spirits high and encourage each other's faith.

Approach 4: The Team Gets Away Together.

A regular practice among football coaches is to have a team dinner together the night before the game. Teammates can see each other outside their usual element, and talk turns to things other than football. This helps the team create well-rounded friendships.

We accomplish the same end by taking semiannual weekend retreats with the ministry leaders and one-day getaways a few times a year. For example, we recently took our staff and their families to a spring training baseball game to show our appreciation for all their help with our Easter celebrations. The ministry leaders, in turn, take their teams on additional retreats. They are primarily for the purpose of building unity. As the leader, don't fill the time with teaching and training and meetings about ministry stuff. Let the team play together and spend quality time together. Deepening team relationships is the core of maintaining morale, period.

Whenever I travel, I try to take someone with me. We have the opportunity to encourage one another in our ministry efforts and deepen our relationship. I particularly try to take young guys who are interning or emerging as new ministry leaders because they will likely represent the next generation of leadership in our church.

Game Planning: Getting Everyone Involved

Ask ministry leaders how they come up with game plans, and they should tell you, "I listen to God." Beyond this, however, leaders have to know what to do with the plans God gives. When and how should they be implemented? Who should be involved? These are just some of the many questions that leaders must answer in order to take the plans on their hearts from inspiration to implementation. Coaching helped me understand how to do this effectively.

Among the planning lessons I learned as a football coach, the primary one is to involve the team as much as possible. If there is one principle that defines how we take God's plans to completion at Christ Fellowship, team involvement is it. There are six steps we use to accomplish this.

Step 1: Have Monthly Elders Meetings.

In these meetings, our team talks about where God wants us to go next. Many elders knew me before the church ever started, and so we trust each other implicitly. We openly discuss the big picture that we see unfolding. The elders do not vote on what is discussed, but come to consensus by prayer on each major consideration. This consensus influences the creation of any new game plan for the church.

Step 2: Hold Weekly Executive Team Meetings.

The proverbial rubber meets the road in these meetings. We have in-depth discussions and reach decisions that give specific direction to the game plan—specifically, we determine how it will affect each existing ministry. To come to these decisions, each executive team member brings the collective input from his team members to ensure that everyone is involved at the outset.

Step 3: Place the Plan Against the Budget.

Most of the initial steps of the game plan are initiated by ministry department leaders as we determine our budget for the new year. This process requires each department leader to evaluate the previous year, set new goals, and then develop a calendar to produce those goals. The calendar is then used to build the budget allotted to the department, which in turn determines what actions can and cannot commence right away.

Step 4: Review the Budgeted Plan Regularly.

Once under way, the game plan is reviewed on a continual basis by the executive director of ministries, who then meets with the leaders of each ministry. The purpose is to ensure that the game plan is being implemented properly and has not slipped off track.

Step 5: Schedule Quarterly Update Dinners.

Every third month, we schedule a dinner for the entire leadership team for the sole purpose of keeping them abreast of the game plan's progress as a whole. All staff members, elders, and key volunteer leaders are invited to these dinners.

Step 6: Annually Report Our Progress to the Congregation.

The game plan is spelled out in detail for the congregation in our annual report. This publication is used to keep the church members aware of our current progress and the direction we expect to take in the coming year. Every active member has a chance to join with the ministry team's efforts in our region by praying and by contributing funds.

In all, the effect of game planning on Christ Fellowship is a team-building one. Because we involve all parties, momentum is sustained, and support is always at a premium. This not only motivates the ministry team to carry out the play with excellence; it adds extra accountability both spiritually and emotionally.

Game-Day Adjustments: Learning as You Go

I learned the value of remaining flexible with plans when I was coaching. I can't remember a single game where we didn't have to adjust our plan in some way. Today, with a church of more than twenty thousand people, that lesson has proved to be invaluable. At Christ Fellowship, change is often our middle name.

We instituted an annual evaluation to determine what we *are* doing that we need to discontinue and what we *aren't* doing that we need to start. Our team understands that a learning approach to each endeavor is necessary. Our team understands that what is most important is loving and serving people, however that is best accomplished.

A good friend once told me that "principles never change but methods always do." It is insightful advice that we've tried to apply by remaining willing to adjust to the growing needs of our people and sensitive to better methods of execution. Here's an illustration.

Recently we launched a Wednesday night service around the idea that we would offer a more in-depth study of the Scriptures. The goal was to offer deeper insights from Sunday's sermons for interested people. The ministry began to grow slowly, but we found that many people who wanted to attend couldn't because they lived too far away, and the midweek drive in traffic made it impractical. That discovery initiated our first adjustment.

We carefully chose to open a satellite location for those who lived too far to drive to the church on Wednesdays. We gave sufficient lead time in order to promote the adjustment to the congregation and then kicked it off in the fall of that same year. The first month averaged five hundred in weekly attendance. The adjustment was a good one.

A few months into this transition, a staff member was exposed to some new research that we felt would help our congregation grow spiritually in a way they hadn't before. A church in California implemented this research into a new small-group strategy, and with this strategy, the church was able to help more people through small groups than we were helping with our satellite site. We were immediately faced with another potential opportunity. Would we stick to the status quo, or make another change?

After further research and much discussion, we made the decision to implement the new small-group strategy just three months after introducing the satellite site. We prepared the ministry team by sending them to observe other churches that were using the strategy successfully. In addition, we brought the designer of the new approach to the church as a temporary consultant. Finally, we informed the congregation of our discovery and newly planned adjustment and gained their support.

The small-group ministry is now thriving. In our first attempt to model the new strategy, we had three thousand adults meeting in different homes. That was considerably more than were involved with the satellite site and a quantum leap over our previous small group ministry. On both accounts, we were glad we made the adjustment because both met our overall goal of helping and growing more people.

In a ministry environment, if you take the time to plan thoroughly, and you are fully aware of carrying out the church's mission, game-day adjustments are inevitable. Personal growth, corporate growth, and new research regularly open up new possibilities.

However, there are three considerations before a ministry should jump at change—even if the team is excited to make the adjustment. At Christ Fellowship, before making a game-day adjustment, we . . .

1. collect all the information we can.

2. get feedback from the paid staff and the volunteer staff.

3. verify that the team is equipped to execute all details.

Once you've taken all three precautionary steps—remembering to bathe them in prayer—game-day adjustments are more apt to be effective. Furthermore, when the goal is more important than the method, game-day adjustments are not difficult to make.

Celebration: Acknowledging God's Work Through the Team

Discovering the role of celebration is as important for a ministry leader as it is for a coach. In both cases, celebration is all about saying "thank you." In ministry this starts with thanking God for His provision and work through your team. Obviously, without His hand, nothing of real value would be accomplished.

From that place, celebration can take on many forms—creativity here is welcomed. But in all, the goal is to recognize the hard work of the team, and celebrate the result.

At Christ Fellowship, we love to celebrate victories, but we're also strategic about it. One of our newest mottoes is, "You get what you celebrate." In other words, if sports are celebrated in your church, your efforts will probably produce athletes; but if spiritual growth is celebrated, your efforts will produce more spiritually mature people.

Here are a few ways we celebrate our goal of ushering in spiritual growth to the people in our region:

- Each Tuesday in our general staff meeting, we celebrate individual victories. Just this week a member of our maintenance team shared about a mission God called him to in the underprivileged neighborhoods of his county. The ministry is now thriving and affects hundreds of lives each month. We celebrate his efforts as an extension of our bigger team's efforts.

- We also celebrate during our weekend services. For example, more than twenty members recently concluded eight months of training for biblical counseling. We held a formal commissioning ceremony in the Sunday service during which we celebrated their efforts and asked God's blessing on their next steps.

- Whenever we send out a group on a mission trip, we also hold a formal commissioning service, whether the trip is one week or one year. Upon their return, we celebrate and give them a public platform to share God's victories abroad with the congregation.

Recently the small group leaders gathered together to celebrate the success of the small group ministry. During this time, a local businessman spoke on the subject of giving. To conclude with a bang, he gave each small group leader a one-hundred-dollar bill, and then challenged everyone to "pay it forward." They were to take the money and see what God could do with it as they invested it into the community. That celebration inspired many more celebrations.

Nearly every following Sunday, small-group leaders shared the amazing stories of what God did with the hundred-dollar investments in others' lives. It was a weekly blessing to the people in the congregation, and it also inspired others to get involved. More important, it served as a reminder of the source and object of our efforts.

I could talk about methods and memories of celebration for another two hundred pages, but I'll leave that to another author. What's important to understand now is that celebration flows steadily when it flows from the heart of God and continues through the heart of the leader to the hearts of the team and congregation and community. It's the most natural, unhindered flow. And let's pray that this flow continues to give us all more reasons to celebrate in the weeks and months and years to come. When it's all said and done, we'll have plenty of time and reason to celebrate some more.

Section III

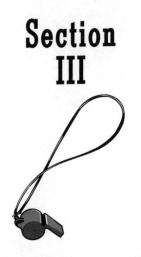

Interviews with the Coaches

9

Up Close and Personal

Maybe it's my age—I don't really take myself too seriously. I think that is pretty important too . . . This is not about me. I was one of two first-year head coaches to ever win a national championship; the other one was fifty-three years ago. I also found out that he was fired. So don't take yourself too seriously.

—COACH COKER, University of Miami
2001 National Champions

Certainly you have to speak and be heard, but you also have to learn to listen. Be sure to listen to the people that you know care about you because you will get ten thousand pieces of advice a day; but you have to ask yourself who really cares about you, your program, your coaches, and your families.

—COACH FULMER, University of Tennessee
1998 National Champions

The idea for this book sprang from my doctoral dissertation, written in 2003, when I originally interviewed all eight coaches. At the time, their insights helped me shape my hypothesis that the chief principles of great coaching provided a creative, effective model for successful church leadership. Since then, others (including, of course, my publisher) shared their desire to see my dissertation in book form and applied for a more general leadership audience. Anyone, they insisted, can become a great leader by becoming a great coach. I agreed and was glad to take their advice on creating this book. I hope it has added to your leadership repertoire.

Here, I share with you some of my original interviews with each coach in anticipation that they will give you more insight into the application of the coaching principles we've already discussed and also provide you with a closer look at the characters of these proven leaders.

Whether or not you root for their teams, I think you will enjoy reading their responses as much as I did hearing them. Without a doubt, they provide more insightful wisdom for leading a team to the championship level.

For the sake of organization and to honor their time, I asked the coaches a similar series of questions in addition to those on the eight topics we've already discussed. Here, in general, are some of the other questions I asked them:

1. What are some of the unique challenges you face(d) at the championship level?

2. What coach made the greatest impact on you, and why?

3. What have you done to move from being a good coach to a great coach?

4. Do you have any other coaching tips that you would like to share with aspiring coaches that we have not covered in this interview?

5. If you summed up your coaching philosophy in one statement, what would it be?

As you enjoy these interviews, ask yourself the same series of questions, removing the direct correlation to the coaching profession when necessary and inserting your leadership endeavor. You may even want to record your answers somewhere. You don't have to be on a football field—or any field for that matter—to think like a coach. In fact, I believe you cannot become an effective leader without first becoming an effective coach. Answering the questions for yourself may move you a few steps closer.

Interview with
Coach Bobby Bowden, Florida State University
1993 and 1999 National Champions

TOM MULLINS: Coach, you've been at it for a lot of years. How did you make the transition to the championship level?

COACH BOWDEN: Well, number one, last year was my fiftieth year of coaching, so I've been coaching for a long time, through a lot of generations. It just seems like in the last ten or fifteen years that we've been able to get to the top level. I suppose the one thing that has meant a lot to us has been the stability of our staff. Up until the last three or four years, we've been able to keep our staff. In fact, I've got a member that's been here for twenty-five years, one that's been here for twenty-six years, a couple of them have been here seventeen or eighteen years, and eventually you begin to lose those. But I think a lot of our success was because of the stability of the staff. I think that's very important for the success of coaching. I think the fact that our coaches stayed with us helped us to be able to recruit better because the kids knew that if they came to Florida State, the guys that were recruiting them were going to probably be coaching them.

TOM MULLINS: What coach made the greatest impact on you, and why would you say that?

COACH BOWDEN: I think the coach that had the greatest impact, and a lot of them had an impact on me, was Bear Bryant from the University of Alabama. I came up under coaches like Frank Thomas (he was in Alabama), Bob Nalen, Bobby Dodd, Willy

Butts, Bud Wilkinson. Those were the guys that were kind of famous as I was getting into coaching. But in 1958, Bear Bryant left Texas A&M and came to the University of Alabama and had a complete new rebuilding job to do there. One year later, 1959, I was appointed the head football coach at Samford University, which is in Birmingham and only forty-five miles away. I came in one year behind him and was able to watch how he brought the Alabama program along. He came in '58, and I think he won his first national championship in '61. Before he left I think he had won about five. I was there for four years and was able to meet and listen to him and talk to all his coaches. I would go down there often to watch him do spring training. That period of four years was probably more influential on my coaching than any other period of the fifty years I've been in it.

TOM MULLINS: When you look back at your great career over these fifty years, what do you think it was that helped you to go from being a good coach to the great coach that you are today?

COACH BOWDEN: I'm not just going to say this because of where you're coming from, but I think my faith in God. It's not the good times; it's getting by the bad times. A successful coach is a coach that can get by the bad times because you're going to have them. Some coaches can't handle bad times. They resign at the drop of a hat when the pressure and criticism get on them; first thing you know they're out. You better be able to handle the bad times, and to me, that's where your faith comes in. That's where you believe there is something a little bit more important than football. I tell my players that football is a priority, but it sure isn't *the* priority. I always feel like coaches that made football the priority in their life have burned out. They're the guys that have cracked up. My faith has saved me.

TOM MULLINS: Your faith and your love for your family?

COACH BOWDEN: Yes, faith and family, God and family.

TOM MULLINS: Coach, just two more quick questions here. Do you have any other coaching tips that you'd like to share with aspiring coaches that we've not covered in this interview? Is there anything else you'd like to share, any other coaching tips we've not talked about?

COACH BOWDEN: Well, one thing I've tried to do that I get criticized for is believing in a second chance for kids (for example, if a kid makes a bad mistake or does something wrong). Now, there are some things they do that I can't help them with. For example, the thing that McPherson got into, that's out of my hands, I can't help him. But if I have a kid that does something bad like breaking a rule, I'll punish him for it. I'm going to punish him for it, but I am also going to give him a second chance. I just don't believe in just throwing them back out on the streets. The popular thing to do is to kick them off the team; the public loves that. "Oh, boy, look how tough he is," but how about that kid? I always felt like you learn by your mistakes, so I'm a second chance man. I'm not much of a third chance man. If I didn't have eighty-five guys, maybe I'd give them a third chance, but I have other guys. I can only let you push me so far.

The other thing I don't think we can do is appease everyone. In football, every coach tries to appease. Everyone thinks this is the right way to do it, and this is the wrong way to do it. I try not to let public opinion sway me either. The public likes one thing; I'd like something else. When I speak at a church or to a pastor, I say, "You know, your job is like mine; half the people like whatever you say, and half of them don't like it. You cannot make them all happy. You simply cannot do it."

TOM MULLINS: One final thing here. If you had to sum up your coaching philosophy in a single statement, what would that statement be, Coach?

COACH BOWDEN: My coaching philosophy would be this: my desire is to win as many games as I can win within the rules, not at the expense of anybody else. When my career is over, I'd like others to say that "he was a winner; he was a winner, and he did it correctly."

Interview with
Coach Larry Coker, University of Miami
2001 National Champions

TOM MULLINS: How would you describe some of the unique challenges that you have faced at a national championship level?

LARRY COKER: Well, for me, being a new head coach, the first unique challenge is putting together a staff and getting everyone on the same page. As you know, it is sometimes difficult just getting two people together. Second is to develop a vision for your group or team and to get them to buy into that vision. Then, I think you have to be realistic with how good you are.

TOM MULLINS: Do you feel that coaching at this level versus some of the other levels that you have coached at has required more of you? Perhaps the difference in being a strong offensive coordinator for a good, solid program and being the head coach of a national championship program?

LARRY COKER: I think the biggest thing is that many of the requirements are things that really have nothing to do with coaching. The outside requirements such as with the media, including print media and electronic media, outside responsibilities such as speaking engagements; I would say that I had a few of those as a special coach, but now I am expected to have several. Other outside responsibilities such as television shows; I tape two television shows a week, which really have nothing to do with us winning or losing a game, but it does indirectly and directly affect our program in regards to recruiting and all the other things that you have to do to maintain a successful program. But I guess the biggest change and biggest outside responsibilities are simply the changes that go along with the job.

TOM MULLINS: You talked earlier about your staff. When you go out to find your staff, what are the top three characteristics you are looking for?

LARRY COKER: One, I look for good people. Two, I look for a person that is knowledgeable. The third is a great recruiter. Sometimes you will have great coaches that really can't recruit. I think you would love to have good people, someone who knows their stuff, and someone who can recruit at this level.

TOM MULLINS: Coach, how would you sum up what the core of your coaching philosophy is?

LARRY COKER: I want to be fair, friendly, and firm with the players. I think, for this program, we have actually had two goals in competing at a high level. First, we are probably not going to win a national championship every year, but we are in a top program that should be able to compete at a high level each year to give ourselves a chance to win. Second, we aim to graduate our players. Those are two main goals for the program.

TOM MULLINS: What advice would you give to people who want to raise themselves to the next level of coaching or leadership?

LARRY COKER: First of all, go to the meetings. If I did anything consistently, it was attending clinics and meetings and taking notes. I really tried to learn from great people and great coaches. Not all of those coaches are from Notre Dame and Miami. I am talking about coaches from Georgetown, high school, wherever. I think that is one thing that I did. I know of several times when I would drive to clinics and there would be people there that would go out at night and just kind of have a party weekend. Instead, I tried to learn from everybody I was around. I often hear people say, "I'm only a junior high coach; I'm only at a small college," but I believe we all have to learn where we are planted.

TOM MULLINS: What other general coaching tips or philosophies would you like to pass on to those that want to learn from your experiences in coaching?

LARRY COKER: I think if I could say one thing that I feel is important, it might be trust; that others can trust you as a coach. Not that you aren't going to make mistakes, but I think some of us need to admit, "Gosh, I screwed up." We were going to have lobster and steak the other night, and it was shrimp and steak. They let me know about that. I said, "Guys, I do know the difference; that's my fault." But again, trust. You have to have trust in them also.

TOM MULLINS: I think that when coaches maintain personal integrity while cultivating integrity and unity among their staff, it will trickle down to their team. Coach, one thing that seems to be very evident about you is that you are a man of integrity. It is very evident in what you and your team have achieved, and I commend you for that. I appreciate that about you.

LARRY COKER: I think that too. Maybe it's my age—I don't really take myself too seriously. I think that is pretty important too. You realize that some people could have a job like this and think they invented it. It is a vehicle that hopefully I am able to maintain and build on, but I definitely don't take myself too seriously. This is not about me. I was one of two first-year head coaches to ever win a national championship; the other one was fifty-three years ago. I also found out that he was fired. So don't take yourself too seriously.

Interview with
Coach Phillip Fulmer, University of Tennessee
1998 National Champions

TOM MULLINS: Coaching at the championship level obviously provides unique challenges that set that level apart from other levels of coaching. As you reflect on that, what are some of those unique challenges that you faced?

PHIL FULMER: Well, I think there are unique challenges, particularly at a school like the University of Tennessee where we don't have quite the recruiting base that our sister schools have. One unique challenge for us would be to bring young people from different areas of the country, convincing them that our tradition, history, and opportunity present itself perhaps better than it would through an in-state school. [Also] I think that we all share the challenge of development, whether it be the social, academic, spiritual, or certainly the athletic development of the young men when they come here.

TOM MULLINS: Coach, who was one of the coaches that made the greatest impact on you, and why?

PHIL FULMER: Well, that is easy for me. There are two people really. [The first is] Coach Doug Dickey, who is actually my boss now and just getting ready to retire. As a high school athlete coming to college with an opportunity to be under him for two years, I was really impacted by him a lot. Also, after my days as a player, in my early stages as a coach, I was fortunate to go to Wichita, Kansas, which is very close to Lincoln, Nebraska. I would go up there a couple times a year to follow Tom Osborne. I have just the utmost respect and admiration for him. His demeanor, the way he runs his program, the way he has kept his staff intact, the way that he has cared for his players, and obviously the way that he has won are all admirable.

I suppose it was both good and bad fortune to play him in '97, the year that he retired. His retirement announcement right before we played them was probably the worst thing that could happen to us. After the game he wrote me a letter, and he said, "Phillip, I really respect what you have done for your team and your program and fans; it won't be long before you win yours." And darn it if we didn't win it the next year!

TOM MULLINS: Coach, as you look back over your career, what did you do to make the transition from being a good coach to the championship-level coach that you are today?

PHIL FULMER: Gosh, I don't know. I think as much as anything it was a maturing process. I mean, you have your work ethic, your principles, your beliefs that you think are going to allow you to be successful, and then it's just a matter of being comfortable with making decisions and managing yourself.

TOM MULLINS: You built a good staff around you too.

PHIL FULMER: I think that the key thing is having good staff and support groups around you. Then you almost become manager or CEO, if you will. I don't really like that part of it sometimes, such as the mail, phone calls, and the things that take you away from the actual game of football, but it is very important to do, and again, I've got a lot of good help.

TOM MULLINS: Coach, if you had to sum up your coaching philosophy in a statement, what would that statement be?

PHIL FULMER: I would say that I am very team oriented. I guess that comes from being an offensive lineman and having to be unselfish.

TOM MULLINS: Do you have any other tips that you would like to share with aspiring coaches trying to improve? Is there anything that you can think of that we haven't covered in this interview?

PHIL FULMER: It's funny that you ask that because we are having our clinic this weekend where we have about four hundred coaches here that I'm going to be introducing. A lot of veteran guys that you see every year come back in order to keep trying to improve themselves, which is always good to see. But you also see a lot of young faces out there that you want to see continue to improve themselves as well. I think that it is like anything else; if you are going to be successful, you've got to put the work into it, the effort. Study—do it diligently; keep learning. You also have to remember that communication is a two-way street. You know that certainly you have to speak and be heard, but you also have to learn to listen. Be sure to listen to the people that you know care about you because you will get ten thousand pieces of advice a day; but you have to ask yourself who really cares about you, your program, your coaches, and your families.

Interview with
Coach Bill McCartney, University of Colorado
1990 National Champions

TOM MULLINS: Coach, what are some of the unique challenges that you faced at the championship level? Is there anything that comes to mind?

COACH MCCARTNEY: When the next opponent would come up and the staff would begin to look at how we're going to attack the opponent and how we were going to defend 'em, we would [often] disagree vehemently. I mean, we would be on opposite ends of the spectrum. One guy would say, "We've got to blitz them or they'll pick us apart." Another guy would say, "No, we can't blitz them. We have to defend them this way." We would go back and forth. See, in coaching we learned that no dissension means no discussion. If you don't have dissenting opinions, you won't have a penetrating discussion; you're not going to unveil all the possibilities. However, what we would do, Tom, is by Tuesday we'd say, okay, this is what we're going to do, and no matter where you were in the argument, you would jump behind what we were doing.

TOM MULLINS: Coach, when you look back at a time in your life when you made the transition from being a good coach to being a great coach, what was it that took place that helped you make that transition?

COACH MCCARTNEY: Well, I never was a great coach. I learned that in football the two most fun jobs were calling the plays and calling the defenses. I patterned myself and fashioned myself as a guy who could do that. But [in the process] what I discovered was that when I empowered somebody else to do that, I really brought out the best in them, and I got maximum performance. I learned to delegate and empower. I was never really a great coach, but I had good people around me, and they were able to become all they could be because I gave them the opportunity.

TOM MULLINS: Coach, are there any other tips you'd like to share with an aspiring coach that we've not covered in this interview?

COACH MCCARTNEY: Well, in terms of motivating and rallying people, I've learned that it's never too late to start over.

TOM MULLINS: To wrap it up, how would you summarize your coaching philosophy in one statement?

COACH MCCARTNEY: It's like the redwood tree. When a redwood grows to maturity, it grows a hundred feet tall, but its roots barely go deeper than a foot or two in the ground. A redwood stands because its roots embrace, grab, and intertwine with each other. That's my philosophy of coaching; you can only do it together.

Interview with
Coach Tom Osborne, University of Nebraska
1994, 1995, and 1997 National Champions

TOM MULLINS: Coach, you have faced some unique challenges at the championship level as you've led teams there three different times. What do you think sets coaching at the national championship level apart from coaching at other levels?

TOM OSBORNE: I felt that it was the chemistry on our football team. You certainly have to have a certain number of good athletes, but there are a lot of teams that have good athletes. You have to have good coaching, but there are a lot of teams that know X's and O's. I felt that the best teams that we had were teams that had a special bond. They were very close, made a fair amount of sacrifice, and had a willingness to forgo personal ambition for team goals. I also thought there was a very strong spiritual presence on our better teams. We had a devotional with our coaching staff every morning at seven, chapel services for our players, and silent pregame and postgame prayer. Most of the coaches I hired in the last fifteen years of my career, well, most of my career, were very strong Christians, which I believe had a positive effect on our players.

TOM MULLINS: It's exciting to know that. Who do you feel has been one of the coaches that has made the greatest impact on you, and why would you say that?

TOM OSBORNE: I learned some things from Dodger Danny and my predecessor, Bob Devaney. Bob and I were very different people. Bob was at times pretty tough on the players, but he also had a good sense of humor, knew when to back off, and had a good rapport. I think that it's important that you be regarded by your players as someone who really cares about them as individuals and that you're not using them or trying to get what you want.

My grandfather, who was a Presbyterian minister, was also a strong influence on me even though he was killed by lightning when I was about ten years old. I hadn't really been around him much, but I knew he was a person of principle. He was a captain of his football team back in 1900, and I think of him as someone who had a strong influence on both my life and my interest in athletics.

My dad was also very interested in athletics. Each of those people had an influence on me. I can't really point to one coach that I can say that I patterned the way I did things after. I think every coach has to be his own person.

TOM MULLINS: When you think back on your coaching career, what do you think helped you make a transition from being a good coach to a great coach?

TOM OSBORNE: First of all, I don't know how I went from being a good coach to being a great coach. We had good players, which makes you a lot smarter. I also think that as time went on, I was probably more willing to discuss the spiritual dimension with coaches and players. I think I was always very spiritually committed since I was very young, but I think I probably let that become more a part of my coaching. I wouldn't preach to them or anything, but I would lay it out there. I would say, "Well, here's where I'm coming from. You guys need to understand this because you need to know what makes the coach tick." I'd let them know that football was important, but that ultimately where they were spiritually with God would probably take them a lot further than athletics would.

TOM MULLINS: Coach, do you have anything that you could share with aspiring coaches that I've not covered in this interview?

TOM OSBORNE: First of all, I think you have to have a clear vision of what your philosophy is. Every year as a coaching staff, we would sit down and write out our mission statement and philosophy, and sometimes they are the same. We thought that was important because we wanted to make sure that everybody was on the same page.

I also think that coaching is teaching. It's really catching people doing something right and reinforcing that. It's much more than chewing people out to get the right reaction. You'd better tell them how to do it right, and then when they do it right, you'd better reinforce it and be positive instead of negative. There are a huge number of teachable moments as a coach; there is great opportunity to influence people's lives. You can be on a very destructive course if you ridicule and humiliate your team. Or you can be somebody who charts a pretty clear course of how to live their lives. Even in adversity, I think you can make a real contribution.

TOM MULLINS: Coach, if you had to sum up your philosophy in a simple statement, what would that be?

TOM OSBORNE: It's important to maximize a player's potential in a way that represents the team well and in a way that honors God. That's the way we did it. We have it written down more strategically, but that's what I've essentially tried to do.

Interview with
Coach Steve Spurrier, University of Florida
1996 National Champions

TOM MULLINS: Coach, what are some of the unique challenges that you faced at the championship level while at Florida?

STEVE SPURRIER: I don't know if there's a huge difference. No matter what level you're on, every coach is trying to get their team to perform at the very highest level they can perform. We try to encourage our players to simply be the best that they can be. With all the parts together, if we have outstanding talent, teamwork, and all those qualities that you must have to have championship teams, we certainly have a chance. But whether I coached at Duke or at the Tampa Bay Bandits in the USFL or at Florida or at the Washington Redskins, there's not a lot of difference between how you coach. You basically try to get the most out of your players, encouraging them to be the very best players that they can be.

TOM MULLINS: What other coach made the greatest impact on you, and why?

STEVE SPURRIER: I tell people that the coach I admire the most is a guy that I have basically only read about, and it's John Wooden, the basketball coach at UCLA. No one will ever come close to equaling the record he has of ten national championships in twelve years. I've read his books and listened to a tape of an interview with him over and over again. I agree so much with his philosophy on life and his philosophy on coaching. I try to incorporate some of his ideas.

As far as other coaches that had a great impact on me, I would have to say my three high school coaches. They were all different people. I had a high school football coach that was sort of laid-back, but he could give us that little emotional talk right before the game. He allowed the assistants to do most of the coaching, but he was well respected and the players loved him.

I also had a basketball coach in high school that was a screamer; he yelled at you. In fact, people say I'm more like my basketball coach than all the others.

We had success in football and basketball, but we never won big. The only sport we won big in high school was baseball. Because we didn't have a baseball coach, a history teacher coached us. He was really an easygoing, laid-back coach. I can never remember him yelling at anybody. But we loved the guy, and we just all had a feeling that baseball was the sport that we were supposed to win in high school. [Under him] we won two state championships in 1962 and 1963 at Johnson City High School. Back then there was no classification, so basically every high school in the whole state entered the tournament, and somehow or another, our high school won two straight championships. Our coach was just a wonderful guy that very seldom ever raised his voice. In fact, I can never remember him raising his voice.

All three were different people, and I think they all had an influence on me.

TOM MULLINS: Coach, what have you done in your career to move from being a good coach to the great coach that you are today? What was it that helped you grow in your coaching?

STEVE SPURRIER: One thing that I think really helped me to be the kind of coach I am now is learning some of the motivational ideas, qualities, and traits of peak performers. I've got some motivational sheets, and one of them is called "Winners and Losers" by Dr. Sydney Harris. He talks about how winners act and talk and the way that losers act and talk. There are about thirty-five characteristics and traits of peak performers.

Another doctor studied human behavior for sixteen years and came up with about nine qualities that [peak performers] all possess. I think these things really helped my coaching career. I learned the mental part of the game rather than just the X's and O's of football.

TOM MULLINS: Are there any other tips that you would like to give to aspiring coaches that we've not discussed today?

STEVE SPURRIER: I'm never good with tips, but the only suggestion I would give young coaches is to try to make the game fun; encourage your players to be the best they can be as both a person and as an athlete. You're never as good as you should be. You've got to believe that you can always get better and that you can always improve as a coach and as players. Your team can always play a little bit better.

TOM MULLINS: Coach, if you had to sum up your coaching philosophy in a simple statement, what would that be?

STEVE SPURRIER: Well, I tell you, Coach Wooden had a description of success that I really like. He said something like, "Success is peace of mind and self-assurance that you have tried your best to be the best that you can be." If you can get everyone on your team trying to be the best that they can be, and you have all the good qualities of teamwork that go along with it, then you've got an opportunity to achieve some great things in sports because it's hard to do that. It's hard to have a lot of people working together trying to be the best they can be while putting team goals first. It doesn't always happen, but that's what I try to do.

Interview with
Coach Gene Stallings, University of Alabama
1992 National Champions

TOM MULLINS: Coach, when you won the national championship at Alabama and through all your years of coaching, what do you feel separated you at that level? Are there unique challenges that you faced at the championship level?

GENE STALLINGS: Staying healthy. The main reason we won the national championship was that the guys that played in the first game played in the last game. You know, that happens most of the time in teams that win. You just go check any team that wins the national championship, and they've still got the same quarterback, they still have the same running back, they still have the key linebacker, the same defensive ends. A lot of teams are just about the same. The thing that separates a lot of them is whether you stay healthy or not.

TOM MULLINS: That's for sure. Coach, what did you do personally that helped you to grow or progress to that level?

GENE STALLINGS: Well, first of all, there's no substitute for knowledge. You know, you can only ride the waves so much. Somewhere along the line, you have to speak with authority. Leadership is the ability to get somebody to do something that they don't particularly want to do that's going to benefit everybody. You'll find a hundred different definitions of leadership, but basically that's what it is. Well, coaching is coaching. It doesn't make any difference what level it is; it's just as hard to get a high school team to perform at a high level as it is a pro team.

TOM MULLINS: Right. What other coach had the greatest impact on you, and why?

GENE STALLINGS: Two of them: Coach [Bear] Bryant because he was obviously the greatest college coach, and Coach [Tom] Landry because he was the greatest professional coach. Both of them had one thing in common; they won, but they won in different ways. Coach Landry's team, in my opinion, was always doing the right thing at the right time. Execution was so important to him. I didn't think the Alabama teams were always ahead of anybody else, but the fact that we had Coach Bryant on our sidelines made the players feel like it was worth a couple of touchdowns. You know the emotional part of it was very vivid there at Alabama.

TOM MULLINS: Coach, just a couple more quick questions for you. For you personally, what do you think it was that enabled you to transition from being a good coach to being the great coach that you were?

GENE STALLINGS: Well, I don't know. First of all, a lot of outstanding coaches don't win. You just may not be good enough to win. A lot of coaches can screw up a good team, but you can see a team that is really well coached, and they just aren't good enough. We tend to judge everybody just by the win-loss record. I judge a guy by what he does with what he has. You know, if you don't have the best guys around but they are still playing like gangbusters, hey, you're a good football coach, [even though] you may be two and eight. And then I've seen some teams that were talented at every position. And they ran about seven and four, and everybody thinks he's a pretty good football coach. The truth of the matter is, he's a terrible coach. That kind of team ought to be winning nine or ten.

TOM MULLINS: I agree. Do you have any other coaching tips that you'd like to share with aspiring coaches that we have not covered in this interview?

GENE STALLINGS: Yes, make them play hard; that's key. They need to go out and play hard. I'm gonna make it simple for you; if you want to move the ball offensively, basically there are two things you have to do. You have to block the right guy the right way. If you block the wrong guy, you're not going to advance the football because you have a missed assignment. If you block the right guy the wrong way, you're not going to advance the football because you had poor technique. But when you break the huddle and go to the line and everybody blocks the right guy the right way, you're going to advance the football because we make it a lot more complicated than it really is. See, we want to win with a scheme, but we're not just going to win with a scheme.

TOM MULLINS: That is so true. Coach, if you had to summarize your coaching philosophy in a simple statement, what would that statement be?

GENE STALLINGS: I've got a philosophy of offense which says when we get the ball, I want a score. My philosophy of defense is not to allow them to move the ball effectively. If I just had a philosophy of football, I'd say get the most out of your player.

Interview with
Coach Bob Stoops, University of Oklahoma
2000 National Champions

TOM MULLINS: Coach, at the championship level in Oklahoma, what are some of the unique challenges that you face?

BOB STOOPS: Well, there are a lot *more* challenges. The more you win, and the more championships you win, the more people want of you. They want a piece of you, want your time, and so it is a challenge to manage your time effectively so that you can continue to do your job and try and win more championships.

You know, outside of that, another challenge is helping your players not take [championships] for granted—don't believe that they just happen and forget to work for it.

And lastly is the challenge that everyone you play is shooting for you. You know, everyone wants to make their name or make their mark by beating the championship team, and so you get everybody's best shot when you play them from that point on.

TOM MULLINS: What coach had one of the greatest impacts on you, and why?

BOB STOOPS: Steve Spurrier, by far, has had the greatest impact on me outside of my father, not only as a person but as a coach. Why? Because of his approach to coaching. His ability to motivate and to lead people and to get the best out of them. I get credited a lot; people talk about the family atmosphere we have here with family dinners on Wednesday nights and just the way we run our program, but really I copied all that from Steve Spurrier. You know, people don't realize that about him, but he is a great family man and is very successful while doing it. He influenced me in coaching and team organization and team motivation and leadership as well as how to be well-balanced off the field. He's strong and has a great faith, and he keeps a great balance between his faith, his family, and his work as a football coach. What I picked up from him is to be sure to keep balance in your life as you go about trying to win games.

TOM MULLINS: What did you do in your personal life to move from being a good coach to a championship-level coach?

BOB STOOPS: I don't know. I don't know that I'm any different of a coach than I've always been. You know, there are a lot of great coaches that haven't won championships, so I don't like to say I'm great. All I've ever done was try to do the very best job I could with whatever I had. Whether an assistant or a coordinator or a head coach, I just constantly tried to do the very best I could in whatever seat I was sitting in.

TOM MULLINS: Coach, do you have any other tips that you would like to give that we have not covered in this interview?

BOB STOOPS: Just what I said earlier. Do the very best job you can in whatever seat you're sitting in. When you do that and then have success in that spot, it leads to something better—advancement—if that's what you want. Some people enjoy what they're doing and stick with it, which is fine also.

TOM MULLINS: If you had to sum up your coaching philosophy in a single statement, what would that be?

BOB STOOPS: My coaching philosophy would be: work hard, earn what you get, strive to be the very best you can, and make sure you enjoy it while you do; otherwise it is not worth doing.

Afterword

I'm grateful you have taken the time to read this book, and I hope you will be the better for it not just in how you lead but in who you and your team become as a result. We (the championship coaches and I) have given you a unique perspective on leadership that is not readily available to most leaders. And my firm belief is that this perspective—inside the huddles and locker rooms of national championship teams, and on the sidelines, at work and at home with national championship coaches—will be one you can take with you no matter what venture you are called to lead.

Like great coaches, all great leaders learn from others—from other leaders and other teams and other followers. This requires maintaining a humble, teachable heart, something each of my interviewees possesses. They taught me much in the process of researching this book—more than I realized I needed to know. And now as you and I part ways to apply these principles to the endeavors that beckon us, my earnest prayer is that *we* would be leaders committed not just to the higher calling of leadership but to the highest calling of loving people. In the end, that's what successful leadership is all about.

Notes

CHAPTER 3

1. Bob Carter, special contributor to ESPN.com, *Wilkinson Created Sooners Dynasty*, Sportscentury Biography, copyright 2004 ESPN Internet Ventures. The full article can be viewed at http://espn.go.com/classic/biography.

2. Statistics from the Bobby Bowden profile written in conjunction with College Sports Online, Inc., and Florida State University, copyright 2004. Full profile can be viewed at http://seminoles.collegesports.com.

3. Ibid.

4. National championship statistics provided by sports history Web site www.HickokSports.com.

5. John Wooden, *Wooden: A Lifetime of Observations and Reflections On and Off the Court* (Chicago: Contemporary Books, 1997), p. 94.

Acknowledgments

I want to thank my wife, Donna, who encouraged me to write this book. Any success in life I may have enjoyed is due to the support of my family. Thank you, Noelle, Todd, Julie, Jefferson, and Mother.

Special thanks to my assistant, Carolyn Master. Without your help this book would not have been a reality.

Thanks to Brent Cole for your guidance and outstanding contribution.

Thank you to all the coaches who have coached me and inspired me to be my best.

Special thanks to the eight national championship coaches who allowed me to interview them for this book.

Special thanks to Dr. Elmer Towns, who has been one of my mentors and helped me tremendously with this project.

Thanks to Dr. John Maxwell for his encouragement, guidance, and support.

About the Author

Tom Mullins coached football for fifteen years and amassed 128 victories at both the high school and college levels. He is the founder and pastor for the last twenty-one years of Christ Fellowship, an evangelical, multi-site church of 20,000 members in Palm beach County, Florida.